Traditional Wooden Toys

their history and how to make them

Cyril Hobbins spent most of his schooldays during wartime, which had a huge effect on the kind of toys that he and most children played with at that time. Many toys were home made by old relatives, or by children themselves from found materials.

Cyril left school at 15 years of age to become a carpenter joiner. After National Service he studied Art at evening classes, going on to design and paint scenery for local theatres, and to produce paintings, as well as working as a joiner.

Between 1973 and 1988 he became a teacher, and then a social worker/manager for adults with special needs, with the emphasis on practical and life-skills.

From 1988 to the present day Cyril has been a tireless researcher and re-creator of traditional wooden toys, becoming well known to many schools and museums countrywide.

Traditional Wooden Toys

their history and how to make them

Cyril Hobbins

Linden Publishing

Traditional Wooden Toys
Their History and How to Make Them
by
Cyril Hobbins

ISBN 10: 1-933-502-10x
ISBN 13: 978-1-933502-10-6

Library of Congress Cataloging-in-Publication Data

Hobbins, Cyril.
  Traditonal wooden toys : their history and how to make them / Cyril Hobbins.
       p. cm.
  Includes bibliographical references and index.
  ISBN-13: 978-1-933502-10-6 (pbk. : alk. paper)
  ISBN-10: 1-933502-10-X (pbk. : alk. paper)
  1. Wooden toy making. I. Title.
  TT174.5.W6H62 2007
  745.592--dc22

                              2006032231

Linden Publishing Inc.
2006 S. Mary St
Fresno CA
www.lindenpub.com
800-345-4447

Printed in Thailand on paper manufactured from sustainable timber sources.

Dedication

To my loving and understanding wife, Glenys, my children and my heirs.

*Suddenly it becomes important to decide what
is a toy...*

*It is a substitute for which
there is no substitute.*

*It exists for its own sake yet it should be
somehow unfinished.*

*It shouldn't be designed to
Teach, yet it should help
You learn.*

Alen Brien
New York Times January 12 1970

From a book entitled *Japanese Folk Toys, The Playful Arts*
by Lee Baten

Acknowledgements

I wish to thank the following for their help and understanding:

My wife Glenys for her proof reading of, and assistance with, my early manuscripts and images; Mr Roger Rolfe my neighbour who carried out the first edit on my early manuscript; Mathew Connolly the text editor; Jane Evans of Stobart Davies Limited for her patience and her sterling book design, proof reading and final editing; Nigel Evans of Stobart Davies Limited for the initial recognition of the potential of this book:

My sincere thanks also go to Joyce and Brain Hall, both of whom gave me much encouragement and a deeper understanding of my role as a professional toy maker in the early days

Contents

"It is an old story, and for some a sad one, that in a sense these childish toys are more to us than they can ever be to children. We never know how much of our after imaginations began with such a peepshow into paradise."

G K Chesterton
Sourced from the book *Peepshow into Paradise* by Lesley Gordon.
Published circa 1953 by G G Harrap & Co Ltd

Foreword

This book aims to introduce you to a wide range of traditional wooden 'folk' toys, dolls and games from around the world, from ancient times to the present day. Folk toys are toys that are created from the heart rather than for profit; they are made by adapting existing designs rather than by slavishly copying them. Many of the toys here have stood the test of time, proving over the centuries their everlasting appeal to all age groups. They always work, they never need batteries and they do not make electronic noises. I almost guarantee that they will never be thrown in the bin, but passed on to family or friends. Please use this book as a resource centre from which you can develop your own unique creations. I accompany all the featured toys with their historical background and instructions on how to make them. I want to encourage *all* of you to have a go!

Cyril Hobbins
Kenilworth

A typical squeeze action acrobat toy.

How to use this book

Boys with egg mill, rattle, whistle and a willow hat. (Ref: Brueghel).

This book is written and illustrated with many kinds of reader in mind. It is full of ideas, facts, instructions and advice. You can dip in at random, or read it right through; it is equally at home in the workshop, on the home bookshelf, in a school or public library, or as a museum resource book. For those who want to make their own versions of the toys featured, the pictures - all supported by clear instructions - are probably the best source of information. For those whose interest is primarily historical, their main point of interest might be the line drawings for context, and the colour illustrations with descriptive text for detail. For schools, the book offers a range of material relevant to many aspects of the National Curriculum in Britain: for infants and juniors the pictures alone should stimulate discussion, making and learning; basic science, and the fact that many of the toys use natural forces, is amply covered in the book. As for older pupils, many of the toys can be easily constructed from card and other found materials, and pupils and their teachers are encouraged to have a go. Safety issues are included, while planning, prototype making and lateral thinking are all encouraged. All levels of skill and the availability (or lack) of tools and materials are taken into consideration. Those thinking of making traditional wooden toys on a professional or semi-professional basis will find the book a useful place to start from: there is a section on setting up and maintaining toy making as a business venture.

Introduction

Why wooden toys? Why bother when children have access to the masses of unbreakable, hygienic and ingenious wonders of today's marketing? My own interest started at an early age. I was born in 1938, just before the start of the Second World War, and at that time toys of every kind were unavailable, the materials being required for the war effort. As the war went on, only a few toy manufacturers were allowed to make toys and games from wood and cardboard, which led to a shortage of shop-bought toys. This was the case in Britain, the USA and Canada. As children of the war, we were almost thrown back to Victorian or Edwardian times: to acquire playthings we had to make them ourselves from found materials using our meagre knowledge and skills. However, grandparents and other older relatives and friends, who made toys in garden sheds, on the kitchen table, or even during quiet shifts in a wartime factory, soon rescued our poor efforts.

They also taught us how to use a penknife, lengths of string, and other suitable materials with which to make our own toys, dolls and games, just like poorer children anywhere in the world. A good example of this resourcefulness was the cotton reel tank, a wonderful toy made from an old wooden cotton reel, an elastic band, a short section of candle and a spent match. When put together in the right way it produced a powerful hill-climbing engine that still amazes and fascinates children today.

Boy on a hobby or stick horse. 18th Century.

Introduction

Boy rolling a hoop (Brueghel).

Over the past sixteen years I have been researching and re-creating traditional wooden toys, dolls and games from around the world and from all periods of history, building up a large library of books and other source materials relevant to the subject. I have also recorded in my notebook, while selling my toys at craft fairs and other events, snippets of information given to me by the older generations, my aim being both to introduce the toys, dolls and games to new generations of children and to jog the memories of older folk so that the things they played with aren't forgotten. The result? A voyage of discovery for some; a nostalgia trip for others.

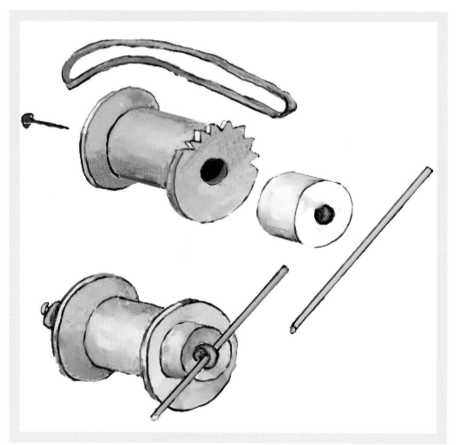

The wonderful cotton reel tank.

Twelve years ago I devised toy-making workshops for schools and museums, and invented a series of 'toykits' - small packs of pre-cut wooden parts, each set allowing participants in the workshops to complete their own working wooden toy. This meant that every child taking part went home with a historically accurate replica item.

Reading through the books in my collection I realized that they were structured in three basic ways: some showed how to make wooden toys, providing plans and instructions and a short essay on tools, materials and finishes, but had little or no additional background information; others were studies of toys from a certain period of history, for example Victorian toys, but with little reference to what went before or afterwards; while a third kind studied specific types of toy for collectors or dealers, for example a collector's book of antique toys, but with no section on where and how the toys were made. Few authors have attempted to bring the whole lot together, until now.

My only restrictions have been to concentrate on traditional toys, dolls and games made from wood - with the exception of rocking horses and dolls' houses, since these two items have received ample coverage in the past. I have concentrated on wooden toys because they are the common thread linking time and place, and because wood is usually to hand in most places.

Bearing in mind that few wooden items survive the passage of time, where is my evidence, you may ask. Thankfully, good quality wooden toys are still available, from countries such as the

Figure on stilts (Brueghel).

Boy with a monkey up a stick.

Czech Republic, where their manufacture is a centuries-old tradition, or through craftsmen who are commissioned to make them, and who sell them at craft events and specialist shops. Also many scholars, scribes and artists have left us with evidence in the form of essays or artwork, all describing or depicting contemporary wooden playthings. This book bears testimony to their contributions. A beautiful painting by the sixteenth-century artist Peter Brueghel, entitled *Children's Games* (see pages 66-67), has been a wonderful inspiration: it depicts at least eighty different toys or children's activities. I want to ensure that the long history of making simple wooden toys is not forgotten, and if only a few readers are inspired to do the same, I will have achieved my objective.

How Toys and Toy Making Evolved

From the beginnings of human history up to the present day, hard-pressed parents have needed toys to keep their offspring amused and quiet - not only for peace of mind but as essential aids for the development of a child's practical, intellectual, emotional and social skills. The earliest peoples had very few or no tools with which to fashion toys, so children would be given anything to hand that would keep them amused and absorbed, such as smooth stones, shells, feathers, pine cones or dried seed pods as rattles, and short sticks - thick for a teething baby to gnaw on, or thin to make all kinds of things, or just to make marks on the ground.

The evolution of woodworking tools has led to a gradual improvement in the quality of wooden toys over time. The earliest humans used found materials from which to fashion most of the items in daily use, and small versions of hunting spears, clubs, bows and arrows, and crudely made 'stick dolls' became the first toys of real significance. They were used in the rehearsal for adult life and survival: boys learned to hunt and fish like their fathers, and the early development of hand-eye coordination gave the miniature weapons great importance. Girls had dolls and clay utensils that helped them to learn how to look after siblings and eventually their own offspring. We might think of these roles as sexual stereotypes nowadays, but guarding the homestead, hunting and fishing were essential for the survival of the tribe.

Hedgerow dolls made from sticks whittled with a sharp knife.

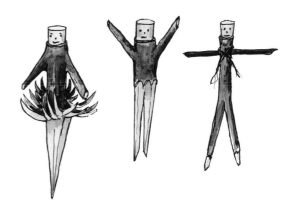

Amazingly, toys have hardly changed since the time of the Ancient Greeks: there is a common thread that runs through their evolution, in the form of a core set of toys, which includes the following types:

- Whip Tops and Spinning Tops
- Hoops
- Fivestones
- Hobby-Horses or Stick-Horses
- Windmills
- Tip-Cat
- Catch Toys
- Stump Dolls or Babies
- Skittles
- Wooden Balls
- Whistles
- Rattles
- Balancing Toys

Throughout history various factors have affected the quality of toys, such as the skills of the toy maker, the materials to hand, and the tools and fixings available. But social factors are important as well. Though wealthy and privileged people have always had the greatest chance of getting the best and the biggest toys, the child of a poor carpenter might have received a beautifully carved hobby-horse on his first birthday, whereas a boy trapped within his father's castle during a medieval siege would have been delighted to receive a simple bent stick with a curved end as a hobby-horse.

In Europe, the earliest wooden toys were made by families and friends, and it was only in medieval times that their popularity grew to the extent that toys were manufactured by

Boy with a whip and top.

craftsmen, who belonged to the new crafts guilds, and who sold them at local markets and fairs, or to itinerant pedlars, who sold them on.

This was the pattern until toy making became a recognized industry in its own right towards the end of the eighteenth century, at first in the forested areas of Germany, where timber as a natural resource was plentiful and cheap. It began as a cottage industry, with individual households and families working together as a co-operative to complete batches of toys for wholesalers, who sold the toys through new mail-order catalogues to retailers across Europe, including Britain, and to the USA and Canada.

More than a hundred years later, during the Great Depression of the late 1920s and early 1930s, many popular magazines and children's encyclopedias published illustrated articles on how to make toys at home. Towards the end of the Second World War German prisoners of war (POWs) were held in camps across Britain, and while they were there some re-created the simple wooden toys that reflected their childhood, culture and tool skills. I am hoping that many of my readers help to build the next step in the evolutionary ladder in the development and creation of traditional wooden toys. Please allow me to help you make your first tentative cuts.

Included in the book are toys dating from the time of the Ancient Egyptians and Greeks, onwards through the Romans and Saxons to the Middle Ages, through the Tudors, Regency and Victorian periods and on to the Second World War and beyond. Each toy is accompanied by its own history.

Tudor children with an egg mill and a hobby/stick horse.

Becoming a Professional Toymaker

Designing and constructing wooden toys in your workshop - or even on the kitchen table - using your own tools can give a great deal of pleasure. The pleasure is increased even further when the finished product is, at last, handed to a lucky child.

Toy making can be a one-off exercise, when time and costs will be of no consequence. The maker has freedom to choose how long to take and which materials and finishes required to make the toy more attractive. (A gentle warning: it is easy to fall into the trap of over-decoration and construction; my advice is to keep it strong and simple. I guarantee that the recipient will be just as pleased.)

You can make a toy as a project in an educational, hobby or club setting, constructing it from a pre-cut kit of parts, or from scratch, then assembled after the study of illustrations and instructions (like those in this book). The instructor will need to prepare everything in advance: tools, materials and instructions, taking into consideration the age and abilities of participants. At first, inexperienced pupils and students should all make the same item; that way it becomes a group project rather than lots of individuals making great demands on the instructor. Later, as confidence and skills improve, individual projects could be accommodated; an intermediate step might be to work in pairs, or fours.

Medieval boys playing battledore and shuttlecock.

You may wish to become a professional toy maker, hoping to make a profit from your efforts. It is not a task to be taken lightly, but with careful consideration and with a realistic business plan it can be achieved. Time costs are the main obstacle when trying to make a profit from self-made items of any kind. Parents, carers and children expect our toys to be cheaper than the lower-quality plastic ones that international companies churn out. These companies also import vast quantities of excellent wooden toys made in China, Indonesia, Peru and the Czech Republic, by taking advantage of cheap labour and low manufacturing costs. You will need to compete in this tough marketplace by ensuring that your products have a unique appeal.

If you are fortunate enough to be able to sell in a tourist area, all the better. I advise against trying to sell through a sale-or-return agreement with shops. The 30-50 per cent mark-up demanded will kill your toys stone dead and your stock will be returned unsold. I strongly recommend that you do not give up your day job during the early stages of setting up, until you are sure of making a living. Selling your toys at craft events, markets and other temporary venues can bring a reasonable return but usually not enough to pay a mortgage. I began by selling from a market stall and stalls at craft events, and during this time I built up my confidence, studied all that I could about wooden toys and gained a good word-of-mouth reputation and a large customer base.

Fortunately, since the National Curriculum was introduced in Britain, the infant and junior

An 18th Century street entertainer with his 'Marionettes-a-la-Planchette' dancing figures: From a contemporary engraving.

curriculum includes the study of toys, their history and development. This leads into the science of forces and the study and making of simple mechanisms. Combining my artistic, woodworking and teaching skills I was able to devise a whole series of practical, hands-on workshops for all age groups, including courses for teachers. My large range of historically accurate folk toys formed the basis of each course; most use one or more forces, and all have a clearly defined history. I devised a wide range of ready-to-build kits, consisting of component parts, instructions and background information. These courses were run throughout central and eastern England, making reasonable profits in the process. I slowly built up a reputation as a leading expert in old-style folk toys, and I now advise museums and bodies such as English Heritage and the National Trust. I also design, devise and research projects for schools' mail-order supplies catalogues, for which royalties are received on profits. Giving talks to interested organizations can also bring in reasonable fees for around two hours' work.

Writing catalogue descriptions or magazine articles can also be a source of income. Use all your wider skills and knowledge to your advantage. Costs can be cut by working from home, but check any planning rules first and be careful not to annoy close neighbours.

You can keep advertising and promotional costs down by buying a business computer with suitable accounting, photo, design/draw and publishing software. This way you can design and print your own leaflets, cards, flyers and posters. I was able to draw all my own catalogue

A street hawker selling windmills 18th Century.

pictures. If you cannot draw use a digital camera to produce JPEG thumbnail prints. Use the computer to design and build your own website, including lots of relevant keywords that will allow search engines to find your site. Send your website address to potential customers and link it to other relevant websites.

Create for yourself a snappy, easy-to-remember title, develop a unique toy maker personality, and wear distinctive clothing in public. I used bright waistcoats, cravats and a leather apron as props, and I even had a replica Tudor costume for working in castles and schools. Every so often, make yourself and your toys a news item worthy of mention in all your local media.

It is essential to make contact with potential customers, to have fun, to interact with families with young children, to be knowledgeable about your subject, and to be willing to network ideas and designs with fellow toy makers - in fact with anyone even the slightest bit interested. Supplying a little history leaflet and a little story or rhyme with the toy also helps sales: a customer may keep it as a reference to order more items later.

Consider selling by mail-order. Should you try selling via Internet auction sites take advice from current users and be honest with your descriptions and prices. You will need to set up a wrap, pack and dispatch table; you will find that eBay and PayPal help with invoices and income via credit card payments as part of the service. Remember that auction bidders situated all over the world will see your toys.

From an old engraving showing how the hobby/stick horse was used in conjunction with a toy windmill. (He holds a toy hawk in his other hand.)

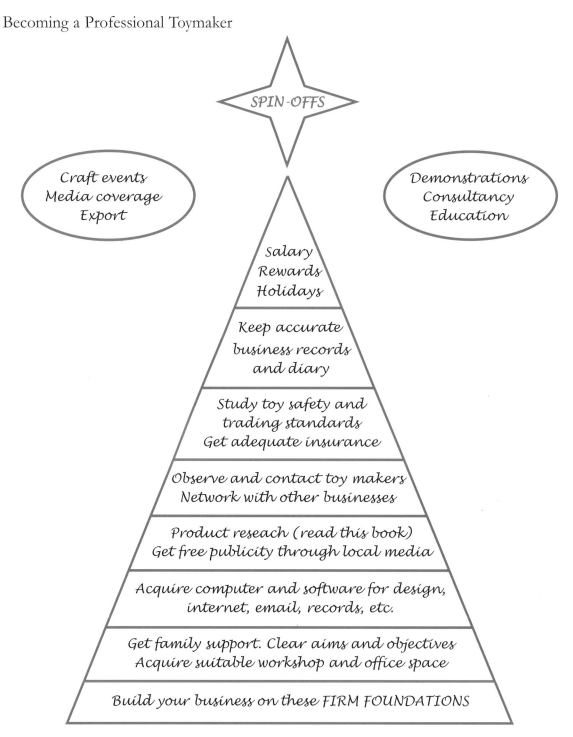

SPIN-OFFS

Craft events
Media coverage
Export

Demonstrations
Consultancy
Education

Salary
Rewards
Holidays

Keep accurate
business records
and diary

Study toy safety and
trading standards
Get adequate insurance

Observe and contact toy makers
Network with other businesses

Product reseach (read this book)
Get free publicity through local media

Acquire computer and software for design,
internet, email, records, etc.

Get family support. Clear aims and objectives
Acquire suitable workshop and office space

Build your business on these FIRM FOUNDATIONS

The business triangle represents a tall architectural structure with strong, firm foundations supporting the upper layers. It also represents the mountain that most new business owners have to climb before achieving both recognition and profit. Finally, the 'spin-offs' draw attention to the rewards that can ensue as a direct result of good business practice.

Tools, Tips and Materials

The mechanisms of the toys illustrated go back centuries, so we cannot acknowledge their inventors. The toys will not work unless the mechanisms are followed, but dimensions and shapes can vary. I encourage you to devise and then make your own unique folk toy that will be treasured by its lucky recipient. That way you will be following very old traditions.

To start, draw the profiles out loosely on to paper, then make card templates, marking the all-important holes for rivets, and so on. When you are happy, draw round them to transfer the profiles on to the timber or board ready for cutting out. If you are making a number of the same toy, you can cut out more than one part at a time. You will need a power scroll saw for this. One way is to pin, glue or tape temporarily up to five layers of plywood or MDF (Medium Density Fibre) board together, mark them out from the master template, ensuring that you drill all marked holes before cutting out. Store stacks of parts in separate boxes, ready for sanding before painting and assembly. Another way to cut more than one part if not using ply or MDF is to draw the profiles on to a thick board. Again, after drilling marked holes first, cut around the profiles with your scroll saw. The thick parts can now be split into suitable thicknesses on the scroll saw or even split off in the traditional manner with a sharp knife or chisel. I have illustrated these methods; please refer to my pictures.

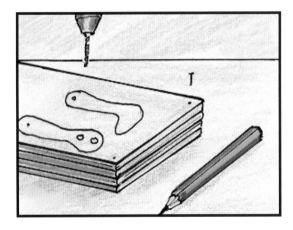

Stack drilling and cutting methods (see text for details).

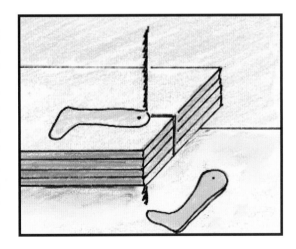

Materials

You can buy timber, plywood and MDF from any DIY (Do-It-Yourself) store or specialist supplier. The more resourceful among you may seek out suitable offcuts from a workshop or factory, or even from a skip, but always ask permission first. A good way of preserving precious timber resources is to use offcuts or to re-use timber to make small items; this way is also much cheaper. Make sure you always check used materials for old nails, screws and fixings before machining them for re-use. To make any of the toys featured in this book, study the relevant illustrations and then draw up your own design using the methods described above.

Decorating your toy

For quantities of wooden toys I recommend using readily available, Trading Standards EN71/3 compliant, water-based acrylic colours and varnishes; they are non-toxic, easy to use, and come in a wide range of colours in primer, gloss, matt and satin finishes. Brushes should always be washed in plain water immediately after use. Sanding and smoothing all parts at the start and in between coats will ensure a good finish. I rarely use a varnish with acrylic colours, to give the best folk toy effect: I use matt or satin colours, then give parts a light sanding with very fine sandpaper. This produces an antique finish with slightly rubbed edges, which is pleasing to both hand and eye. A light application of clear wax with a brush, then rubbed with a lint-free cloth, gives an attractive light sheen and a toy that is a pleasure to hold.

If you want a toy to have an authentic antique

A boy using a bat and trap or trap ball.

look try decorating it with a pyrography pen. In the past, many wooden items would be simply decorated by drawing the designs with a red-hot poker or a wire rod held in a wooden handle; the pattern or picture could be left plain or coloured then waxed or varnished for protection. Nowadays, pyrography pens are electric and come with transformers that control the heat going to the business end, in a similar way to an electric iron. A whole variety of designs and patterns can be permanently applied very quickly; rubber stamps or tracing can help those who lack drawing skills.

Fixings and Adhesives

DIY stores or mail-order companies are the best sources for nails, pins, screws and adhesives required. Should you wish to make a quantity of toys, a power tacker/stapler would be a useful addition to the toolbox. Always remember that any nails or screws used on toys should be child-safe, and not used if there is any way that a child could expose sharp points at any time.

You will note from my drawings that most loosely jointed toys have looped wire rivets as pivots. These are easily made from standard galvanised wire, rolls of which are available from DIY, hardware and farm stores. The size of the toy will dictate the gauge required, but generally wire that is 2mm-3mm in diameter is satisfactory. To make a rivet use a pair of long-nosed pliers to form a small, neat loop at the end of the wire roll; a twist of the hand is all that is required. It is important that the end of each loop meets up neatly, ensuring that no potentially dangerous hook is formed. The cut rivets can be stored in a tin or jar.

Medieval boys whipping a large spinning top on a clay mound.

How to make and use wire rivets.

17

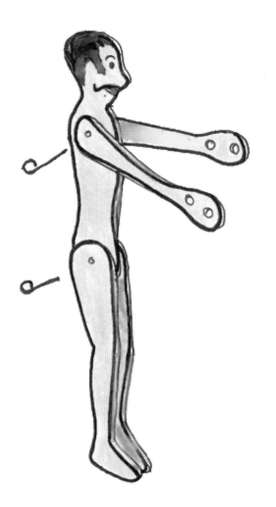

Acrobat assembly details.

To assemble a toy, push a rivet through the pre-drilled holes, then cut it off if it is too long, leaving 10mm-12mm of wire to form the other loop. Hold the toy up, and then swing it back and forwards to ensure that the parts move smoothly; if not, a little adjustment of the loops can be made with the pliers. For general use, the standard white, waterproof, woodworking glue is fine; for metal to wood or for extra-strong joints, I advise a two-mix epoxy resin (Araldite), and for leather or cloth to wood, a rubber-based contact adhesive (Copydex). Always follow the manufacturer's safety and other instructions when using any glues or adhesives. Rather than drawing round another designer's templates, tracing or using detailed plans, follow the example of the toy makers of old by using your eye and imagination to create your own version. The basic mechanisms can be easily transferred or mixed and matched.

Safety Note

It is advisable when constructing any toy for use by children (particularly if you intend to sell it) that you follow current European toy safety legislation, details of which are available in most reference libraries. There should be no sharp points, splinters, rough or sharp edges on a finished item. Likewise, use non-toxic paints and varnishes, and ensure that no long cords or small parts can injure or choke a child. Even though it is a folk toy, it must be made to meet these very sensible standards. There are special rules for toys intended for babies and for larger ride-on toys not covered in this book. For toy makers in the UK, the Trading Standards Institute gives good advice. See www.tradingstandards.gov.uk.

The Toys

Each description is accompanied by my own coloured illustrations clearly depicting examples of the toy and how it is constructed. After you have made one or two of the toys illustrated you will be able to adapt and alter the designs to create your own version. I have deliberately omitted dimensions, tools, materials and cutting lists, because I strongly believe that any creator of folk toys should use those available at the time. You could make any one of these toys using a good penknife, but access to suitable hand and power tools will make the task quicker and easier. Tool skills develop with practice; I recommend taking a short course at a local college or evening class. A fertile imagination combined with a little lateral thinking also helps.

Hobbin Dobbin a, no tangle, two string puppet of my own design.

Animated Toys

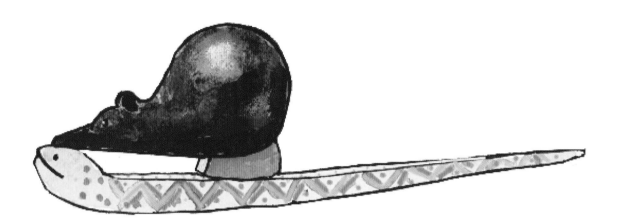

Ancient Egyptian snake and ichneumon toy rattle.

The Ancient Egyptians can almost certainly take the credit for being among the first civilizations to devise a whole set of animated toys. Ancient Egyptian society might have had slaves and tyrannical Pharaohs, but Egyptians loved their children. You can find examples of their early animated toys in museums and specialist collections all over the world. Remember that many realistic models made by the Ancient Egyptians were intended as grave goods, to accompany a dead person into the afterlife. However, the toys described here were probably meant to be used by children.

The Ichneumon (Mongoose) and Snake consists of a snake whittled from a stick. Just behind its head an upright bracket is dowelled in; on this is pivoted a carved ichneumon or mongoose. When you hold the snake by the tail and shake it the little ichneumon appears to bite its neck. Apparently the ichneumon was kept as a family pet - and to keep potentially dangerous snakes away from the home. It is an easy toy to reproduce from my illustration.

The Lion or Tiger, the Crocodile and the Grinder are unique in that they were among the first wooden toys to be animated by pulling and releasing a cord. The first two both have a clever hinged lower jaw that has rows of sharp little teeth consisting of tiny wooden pegs. A light tug on the cord and the jaws snap shut in a very realistic manner. You can imagine the fun and storytelling surrounding these delightful items.

Ancient Egyptian toy lion with cord operated jaw.

Though they are harder to carve than the snake, they are well worth the extra effort. Study the drawings carefully and you will find that they consist of very basic shapes. If you are not able or inclined to carve, you can still make similar toys from simple blocks of wood or even card.

The cord passes through the nose of both creatures; it is then glued and wedged into the front of the hinged lower jaw. The lion is glued and pegged on to a crude wooden base while the crocodile is free standing. On completion you can give both toys tiny bead eyes that are glued into pre-drilled sockets, then the whole is painted in washed-out earth colours and finished off with a light rub with beeswax.

Ancient Egyptian toy crocodile with pull-cord jaw mechanism.

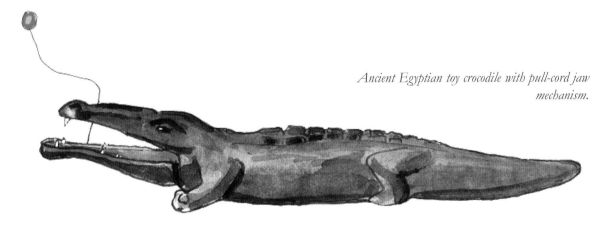

The Grinder is slightly easier to fashion but more complicated to assemble, owing to the larger number of parts. The toy is meant to be a slave hard at work grinding grain for her household. The delightful original of this toy is kept on display in the Leiden Museum in the Netherlands. To make her, first cut a rectangular, flat base from board, and then fashion a wedge-shaped block that is dowelled and glued at one end of the base (see illustration). Carefully cut the torso and head of the figure and then carve them into the distinctively Egyptian profiles,

Ancient Egyptian animated figure grinding corn, note the pull cord action.

complete with tall, pointed headdress. The long, thin, wedge-shaped legs are slightly larger all round than the very similar arms. Drill the tops of the limbs and the body to take thin wooden dowels (I use cocktail sticks or sections of bamboo skewer). The diameter of holes in the body must be just large enough to allow free movement. Next, shape a block of wood to look like a large grinding stone or lump of dough; drill this to take the hand ends of the arms. Drill two similar holes into the base for her legs, and one just behind through which the cord will pass. I suggest strongly that you make a working prototype before making a quantity: this way you will iron out any problems.

Drill the bottom end of the grinder's torso to take a thin cord that is first tied and then glued; pass the cord through the hole in the base, then tie and glue a wooden bead as a grip. When the cord is pulled then released, the figure should repeatedly bend from the waist while her arms, holding the grindstone, will slide back and forth on the sloping block. The grinder is a wonderful toy to observe in action; it certainly brings to life the sheer backbreaking work done by thousands of slaves every day. Ask yourself how long would it take to grind the weekly flour required for a whole family by that method?

The little **farm animals** made by Ancient Egyptian toy makers are not animated as such, but they are delightful nevertheless. Like all toy animals, they can be pushed and pulled around a model farmyard or taken out to graze or to work in imagined fields. Simple blocks of wood were crudely carved into the basic profiles, then decorated with patches or spots of earthy

Ancient Egyptian toy cattle on simple block stands.

The Acrobat has become a worldwide favourite; a simple but effective mechanism that is thought to have originated in China many centuries ago.

There are many variations, but all use the same mechanism; animal as well as human profiles can be used. Some makers use well-known characters from literature and films, such as Mickey Mouse and Popeye. Many commercial toy makers have produced acrobats, but my particular favourites are the ones devised by the amateur toy maker having access to only basic tools and materials. They usually have a charm all of their own, having been decorated with any household paints to hand at the time. Like the Pecking Chickens, the acrobat was a favourite of POWs.

colours. Each one would be drilled at the four corners to take thin dowel legs. (See also the Ancient Egyptian Paddle Doll.)

The origins of the toys that follow are difficult to pinpoint, not only in terms of place but also in time. Most seem to have Far Eastern connections, only to resurface all over the world in later times.

A typical squeeze acrobat toy fully assembled.

The Acrobat has remained popular in Europe since the early nineteenth century and consists of a sideways-facing, jointed figure suspended loosely from a twisted cord tied between the uprights of a tall H-shaped wooden frame. When the bottom of the frame is squeezed and then released the cord untwists, thereby making the figure somersault over the string, the loose joints ensuring a variety of random and amusing actions.

The all-important H-frame can be constructed in more than one way. Please refer to the illustrations for the many varieties I have discovered to date. To ensure that the toy works efficiently it is important that at least one of the uprights has plenty of play where it pivots on the short crossbar. Actual dimensions are left up to

Examples of alternative H frame design for squeeze acrobats, all have a loosely pivoted side.

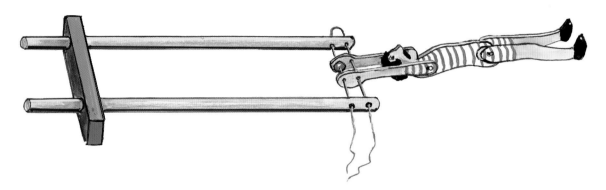

How to string a squeeze acrobat toy.

the maker, but it is good to remember that toys are meant for use by children and need to be designed to fit into a medium-sized hand. You can cut the figure from thin ply or MDF or, after drawing all parts in profile on to a straight, grained, solid board, cut the profiles then slice them down the grain with a sharp knife, chisel or saw. (A scroll saw makes short work of this.) The frame needs to be light but strong, so hardwood dowel or suitable strip is recommended. All parts need to be sanded well and then decorated to suit; assemble them as shown in the diagrams, using looped wire rivets (See Tools, Tips and Materials.)

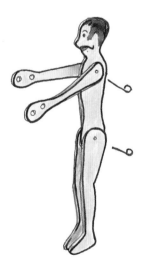

Assemble the acrobat figure loosely with wire rivets.

You can make **Pecking Chickens** in many different ways: essentially, it has a lightweight pivoting neck and tail, the bottom ends of which are fastened to a cord attached to a weight. When the weight is allowed to swing around in circles the bird or birds peck greedily at the painted corn. You can shape the plywood base of the toy like a table-tennis bat with a group of four to six chickens facing inwards. Alternatively, you can mount a single chicken on a long narrow board as shown. A little experimentation with cord lengths and weights is recommended for best results.

Many variations of the Pecking Chickens toy have been made since the early nineteenth century, from the toy making co-operatives in Germany. Their popularity rose again in Britain during and just after the Second World War thanks to German POWs. They are currently available from both Russia and the Czech Republic. The Russian versions are particularly attractive.

Two examples of weight operated pecking birds.

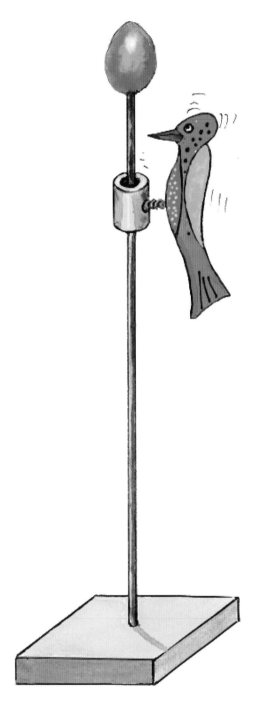

A falling woodpecker gravity toy that vibrates as it descends.

The Falling Woodpecker demonstrates beautifully natural forces at work: just push him up to the top of his tree and then give him a slight tap to start him on his downward journey. The vibrations of the spring create intermittent friction that, combined with gravity, causes him to fall in a comical series of jerks. The illustrations show two ways of making the toy, one with a spring made from wire that has been wrapped around a nail having a slightly larger diameter than the welding rod upright. The other uses a bead that has a hole, also drilled just oversize; the short length of curtain wire (plastic cover removed) is glued in holes in the bead and the chest of the wooden bird. The upright can be made from any metal rod such as welding wire or an old knitting needle. Wooden dowel works too, but is easily broken. Again, a little experimentation with a prototype will iron out any problems; experiment also with falling figures or insects.

The Pantin is a flat, wooden, front-facing figure with loosely jointed limbs that all rise together when a central cord is pulled. Making a pantin is reasonably easy if you follow the diagrams; the tricky bit is to get all the limbs operating at the same time when the cord is pulled. On a suitable board mark out, drill and then cut out the front and back body sections; they will be exactly the same if you stack-cut a pair at a time. Go on to cut all the limbs as shown; the simplest models have no joints. The loose joints at knees and elbows can all be cut on the scroll saw; the round end of a sander belt can also be used to shape the tenons. The limbs need to be rounded off by basic carving or by shaping on a sanding belt. Drill suitable holes at the top ends of all limbs to take the cord ends and glued wedges (cocktail sticks or split slivers). The main pivots holding the limbs to the body can be of wood or wire. Do not forget to cut and drill a spacer block or blocks to hold the torso at the back and front, apart just enough to allow the limbs to swing freely. Cut the head from a flat board or turn it on a lathe then shape it afterwards with a sharp chisel or penknife.

An 18th Century street vendor with a display of pantin/Hamplemann toys.

A fully assembled Pantin/Hamplemann toy.

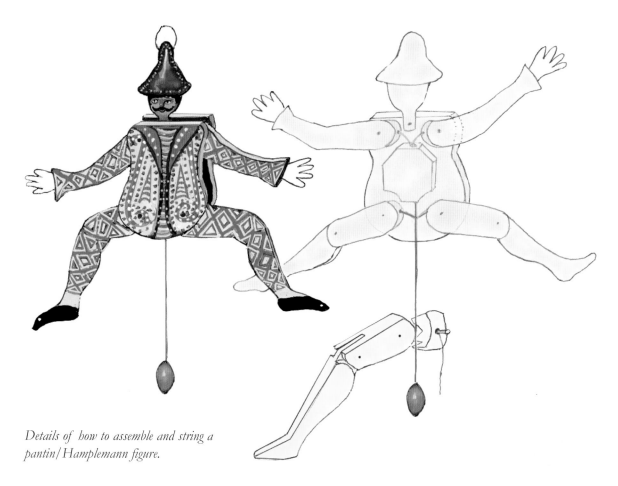

Details of how to assemble and string a pantin/Hamplemann figure.

When you have shaped and decorated all the parts, assemble the limbs first, then fit them over the pivots on the back half first. The top end of each limb should have a length of thin cord glued and wedged tightly into the top hole. Feed all four cords down through or between the spacer block(s) then tie them all together where they meet; then tie the central cord that will operate them all. Before gluing the two halves of the toy together give the cord a few gentle pulls to ensure that all the limbs rise as one. You can also turn the whole thing on a lathe: the assembly methods will be the same in each case.

The Pantin first became popular in mid-eighteenth-century France, but it probably originated well before that in Germany. There are many contemporary illustrations of pantins in action, and as the pantin craze swept through the fashionable Europe of the time, particularly Paris and London, it was stated that 'no home should be without one'. Most pantins were crudely modelled on Mr Punch, or as brightly uniformed soldiers, and a great number were made to represent famous and infamous public figures, especially politicians. Sadly, this eventually led to the toy's downfall: so enraged were ill-natured members of the gentry at being lampooned that they soon spread the lie that the toys were harmful, 'because the women, under the lively influence of this continual jumping, were in danger of bringing children into the world with twisted limbs like the pantins', to quote a contemporary source. So the bright, cheerful and amusing pantin soon went out of fashion. Happily, he resurfaced in Victorian times and remains popular to the present day. The toy is known as a Hampelmann in Germany and Jumping Jack in Britain (not to be confused with the springy, jumping Jack-in-a-Box).

Toy makers in France, Germany, Czechoslovakia and Russia manufactured pantin-like toys of animals and birds as well as the human figure. Russian versions were beautifully carved from unpainted lime wood. Others, instead of being cut from flat boards, had the limbs turned on a lathe.

One of my most popular pantin-type toys is a little wooden owl (it could be any type of bird) which is simple to make, as only the two wings need to operate when the cord is pulled. In my collection there is a skilfully carved owl from Russia; when the cord is pulled, both wings rise and his beak opens. The basic pull/gravity mechanism of the pantin could be used elsewhere - on a simple wind-driven whirligig, for instance.

The Falling Fish is a folk toy similar to those sold by street vendors in many developing countries. It works in exactly the same way as the falling woodpecker except that the pair of fish (can be insects) vibrate down two tightly stretched thin cords that are tied to a wooden frame as shown, instead of a dowel.

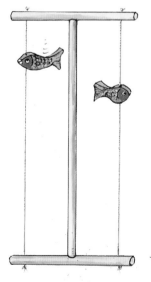

A falling fish gravity toy from India, the cords are stretched very tightly.

Posable toys are included in the animated section because they have tightly jointed limbs that can be repositioned. The Little Dog and the Little Donkey featured here are easily made from scraps of wood found around the workshop. The wire for the rivets needs to be slightly thicker, and the loops need to be carefully hammered flat to ensure stiff posable joints. Remember that dogs and donkeys are not the only animals that can be made in this way: have fun with different breeds, or make a complete zoo. Sizes are left entirely up to you; photocopying suitable pictures will give you accurate cutting profiles that you can enlarge to suit.

Wooden dogs with stiff poseable joints.

Wooden donkey with Poseable joints (like many toys it is ideal for story telling).

The Ancient Egyptians, Greeks and Romans all produced similar posable wooden dolls and animals. Victorian children also enjoyed playing with a wide variety of posable wooden figures and animals; many toy manufacturers in the USA and Europe produced them in vast quantities. Most famous among the toy manufacturers was the family of Benjamin Potter Crandall, father and sons who between them created a whole range of beautiful wooden toys between the 1840s and 1890s. Apparently, they used offcuts from their box-making factory. The toys were all made from thin board covered in printed-paper lithograph designs. These patented toys featured tiny tongues and grooves so they could be stacked and joined together on sturdy grooved bases. Most famous among these was a complete model of John Gilpin and his horse, the whole toy illustrating brilliantly the comic ballad of the unfortunate linen draper by the eighteenth-century English poet William Cowper.

Around 1870 the German toy maker Albert Schoenhut emigrated to America, where his business quickly expanded, producing an eccentric range of posable wooden animals and figures. They were beautifully designed and unique, all parts being lathe-turned and drilled through to take a strong elasticised cord that held them tightly together. Among the best-known is the Schoenhut Circus, which included a complete set of animals and performers along with a jolly ringmaster. Schoenhut was also well known for his miniature wooden pianos.

Many other companies produced similar items, all of which are very collectable today. During schools workshops I have noted that children of all ages really enjoy playing with these wooden counterparts of the modern (plastic) Barbie and My Little Pony toys. The wooden versions are much cheaper and much more attractive. The parts can be individually cut or stack-cut depending on the quantity required; the illustrations clearly show how attractive the finished toys are. I make them plain so that children can use crayons or paints to create their own wooden pets. A cardboard box is soon transformed into a stable or kennel; plastic bottle tops will suffice as food and water bowls. I have watched groups of children completely absorbed in making up stories and scenarios for their wooden friends.

I found the very amusing **Ita Sumo toy** completely by chance while browsing the Internet for ideas. It dates from eighteenth-century Japan: the stylised profiles and decoration are typical of that country. Cut a pair of hefty sumo wrestlers and their limbs from any suitable thin board; the limbs can be slightly thinner than the bodies. Note that the two figures share the same pair of interlinked arms that have central holes to take a short length of thin dowel or bamboo. All the joints need to be loose enough to enable the figures to turn right over within their linked arms; make the bodies about 7cm tall. You can simply chalk a suitable ring on to a floor or thin board. The operator holds the end of the dowel between finger and thumb ensuring that one wrestler has at least one foot on the ground at any time. Manipulating the

A traditional 'Ita-Sumo' toy from Japan.

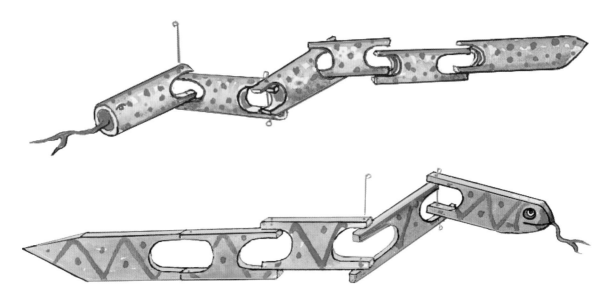

Two ways of constructing a wriggly snake toy.

wrestlers into a whole variety of throwing positions can be lots of fun.

Wooden Snakes that wriggle can be made in two ways. The simplest is to cut a narrow strip of wood into sections that fit together rather like a bicycle chain, as shown. The ubiquitous wire rivet holds them together. Using a length of bamboo cut in a similar fashion is a little more difficult but a more realistic round snake is the result. They can be found as street toys in India and China. In parts of South America toy makers produce excellent wooden snakes, after carving the snake they split it vertically lengthways into two halves and then glue a strip of strong rubber (ex-tyre inner-tube) or thin leather between them; when the glue is dry, they mark the snake into sections and use a sharp saw to cut carefully just down to the rubber core. Then they paint and varnish the snakes to make them look natural. When held by the tail the snakes wriggle in a very realistic way. Lizards and other reptiles can be made in the same way.

The Twirly Doll is based on a folk toy from India sold by street-vendors. It is made totally from bamboo sections. When the dowel on which she is fixed is twirled between a forefinger and thumb her arms and legs fly upwards - an elegant way to demonstrate centrifugal force at work. The illustration can be easily followed.

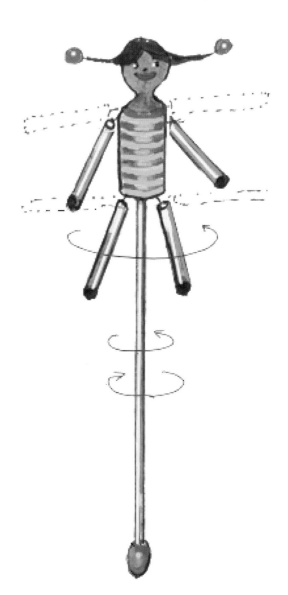

A twirly whirly doll, a street toy from India with a centrifugal action.

The jumping queen another Indian street toy that utilises a simple spring board (see page 37 over).

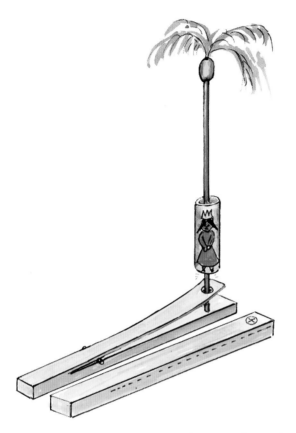

The Jumping Queen is another toy from the same source, and there are many variations depending on the skills of the toy maker. Rip carefully a long block of hardwood two thirds down by hand or on a band or scroll saw, as shown in the diagram. The strip left should be 2mm-3mm thick. Drill a hole at the cut end to receive a thin dowel or branch. The hole in the bouncy strip should be drilled again to leave plenty of play. Glue the dowel into place. The Queen (could be a King) is fashioned by making and gluing a paper tube as shown. When it is dry place it over the dowel, and then glue a wooden bead at the top, which represents the queen's bedroom; a few coloured feathers will add colour and movement.

The Jumping Queen Story

Once upon a time, a very rich queen demanded that a new palace be built. At once, all the best craftspeople set to work on the project. After many months all was finished, and the delighted queen was taken on a grand tour of all the downstairs rooms, but when the grand party went to go upstairs, there were no stairs. Now the queen was angry and tired: just how was she going to get to bed?

All the architects and builders were summoned; the queen threatened them all with dire punishment if a solution was not found at once. All kinds of solutions were suggested … A ladder? NO! … A rope to climb? NO! … A lift? NO! The queen became angrier and angrier. Then, the court magician suggested that he might be able to help by using a small section of his magic wand. The queen agreed. He carefully cut the end off the wand, muttering magic words as he did so. Then the crowd stood back in awe as he prised up one end of a highly polished floorboard under which he placed the magic stick.

The impatient queen just could not wait: she jumped on the end of the board and was immediately shot up towards her beautiful new bedroom. After a few more jumps she landed right on to her feather bed. Everyone clapped and cheered, and the queen smiled broadly as she said goodnight. Don't you wish that you had a magic wand under your floorboards?

Yet another street toy from India is the **Animated Insect**, which could be a butterfly, moth or dragonfly. A large paper or lightweight board insect with a pair of flexible wings is fixed centrally on top of a thin dowel or straight stick. A large wooden bead (or section of hollow bamboo) has a pair of wires connected to the wings, and when the loose bead is pushed and pulled up and down on the stick the insect's wings flap as if it is flying. This is another wonderful story toy that demonstrates links and levers working together. A second bead or bamboo section is fixed to hold the wings horizontal at rest and to prevent the slider from falling off. The flying insect is an ideal project for school or group drama productions.

A flying butterfly push-pull action toy (India).

The **Expanding Scissors Toy** was a great Victorian favourite, consisting of a row of wooden crosses all joined together at the ends. All the joints are riveted to move stiffly; when the end pair of crosses are opened or closed like scissors all the rest do the same. It is a complete set of links and levers - an ideal science toy. You can make the toy from any suitable hardwood; this kind would have a company of soldiers, or a troop of dancers, one fixed at each joint. When you operate the mechanism the soldiers retreat

A set of Victorian soldiers mounted on a set of scissors action strips.

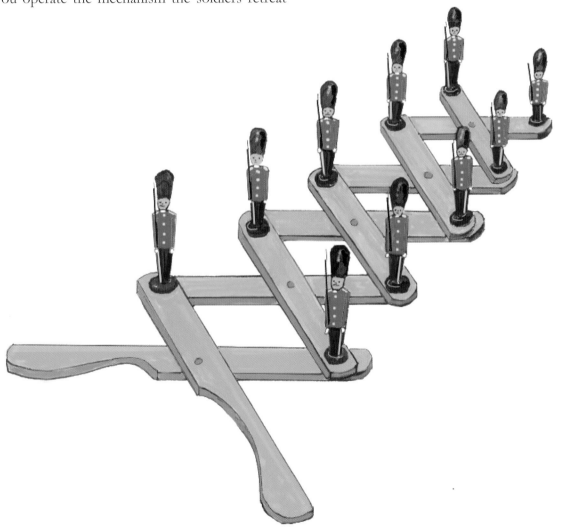

A scissor action tickling toy (sometimes given as a fairground prize).

and advance, or the dancers perform various moves, pivoting as they go. You might have seen a much smaller, cheaper version as a fairground prize, or at a street market. These consisted of the same mechanism made from thin slips of softwood such as pine. The ends of the first cross might have been cut and drilled the same shape as scissor handles; the two at the furthest end might have had colourful feathers to tickle someone's nose as the toy expanded. Others might have had lobster-like claws or even paper spiders - in fact, anything that was scary or fun. The scissors toy can also be made from flat wooden lollipop sticks or even strips of stiff card, pivoting on bifurcated paper-fasteners.

Tumbler Toys do exactly that: they tumble over repeatedly as they roll lazily along horizontal or sloping double beams. When suspended, the basic C shape should hang so the feet are level with the bars; a slight twist to the wire or a gentle tap forwards will start it rolling. A very shallow bend in the axle wire may help it along. As always, I recommend that a working prototype be made first to iron out any problems.

You can construct the bars as part of a simple frame as shown, or a taller frame - with short bars projecting inwards from both sides. Give them a slight slope and the toy will roll, passing from one to the other in an amusing way. Alternatively, place a pair of very long bars on wooden blocks (or even on books) so that your little toy can have a long run. The illustrations make things clear. Gravity helps pull the toy down a slope, helped by centrifugal force created by the eccentric flywheel effect of the turning C shape.

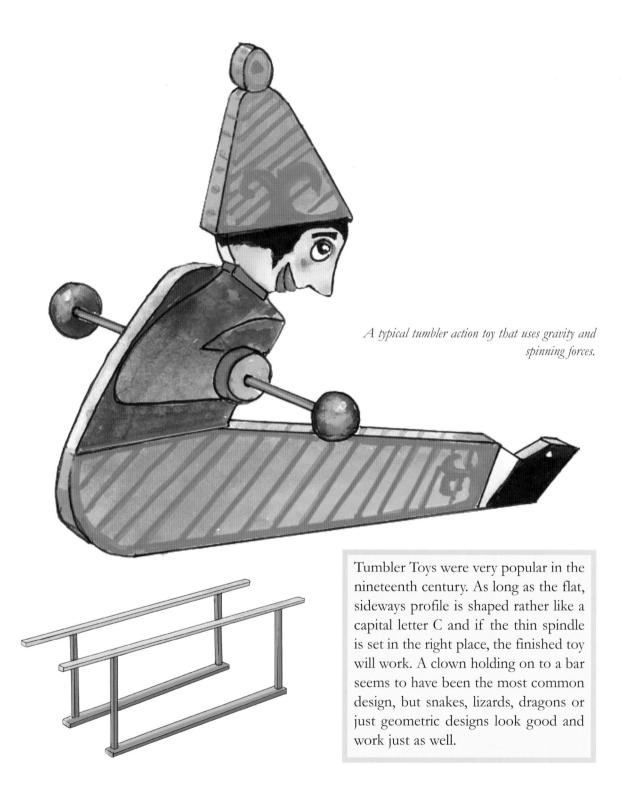

A typical tumbler action toy that uses gravity and spinning forces.

Tumbler Toys were very popular in the nineteenth century. As long as the flat, sideways profile is shaped rather like a capital letter C and if the thin spindle is set in the right place, the finished toy will work. A clown holding on to a bar seems to have been the most common design, but snakes, lizards, dragons or just geometric designs look good and work just as well.

The Centrifugal Roundabout has instant appeal to infants; it also clearly demonstrates centrifugal force, gravity and friction. It is made from two circles of board, a length of 8mm dowel, a bead and two lengths of narrow ribbon or strong cord, short lengths of 6mm dowel and four more large beads. One circle forms the base; it can be larger in diameter and slightly thicker than the other if wished. Drill a hole in the centre of the base in which to glue the central 8mm dowel; drill a bead or wooden ball likewise, and this will eventually hold the cords in place at the top. Next, drill four opposite holes in the upper disc, as shown, to take the cord; now drill four more to take the 6mm dowel in between. Lastly, drill a 15mm hole in the centre.

Sandpaper, then decorate all parts to suit, then assemble as follows: glue the tall dowel into place, and then put the upper disc over it. Next, put a dab of glue on its top, and lay the ribbon or cord crossways in the glue; push on the bead to hold them in place. Now for the tricky bit: use two blocks (spring clothes pegs?) to raise the upper disc slightly, then use cocktail sticks and glue to wedge the cords so that it hangs exactly level when the blocks are removed. While that glue is setting, glue the four beads on to the short dowels: these are your roundabout riders. Paint or draw faces as shown; the addition of nylon hair wigs adds to the fun; glue them into place on the roundabout.

When all is dry, give the roundabout a firm push; it will revolve, twisting the cords down the central dowel as it does so. You will notice that it also rises, and then falls, rotating the other way.

A centrifugal/gravity roundabout toy with a back and forth rotating action.

This action is repeated until the friction on the central dowel uses up all the energy stored in the flywheel. A much more complicated version could be devised that has cut-out animals or vehicles around the edge. The larger this toy is made the better it works.

Rocking Animals and Figures are very amusing, and many variations have been around since Victorian times. They are simple to make from scrap timber found in most workshops, and consist of a curved base on the top of which is glued a flat, cut-out animal, which can have a wobbly head and tail pivoted as shown. When the toy is sanded, decorated and assembled a gentle push sideways will send it rocking back and forth. The rocking cow illustrated is just one example. Gravity will ensure that the head and tail sway in the opposite direction in a very amusing manner. Rocking animals and figures can also be made from stiff card: the lower curved base would need to be filled with sand or modelling clay to give it substance. Lots of fun can be had inventing variations; for example, a Harry Potter wizard complete with wand would work really well.

A good example of a rocking toy with swinging tail and head.

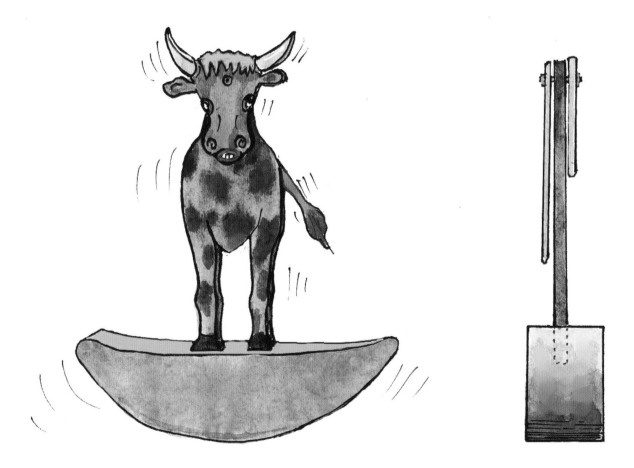

Balancing Toys

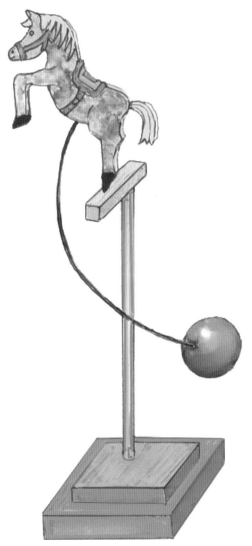

A pair of single weight balancing toys, very popular in Victorian times.

The secret of every balancing toy is weight distribution: the added weights or the main mass must be placed well below the centre of gravity where the balancing point of the toy touches the table or stand. The illustrations make this clear: the horse and the boat (page 45) have a single weight suspended from a bent wire rod, while the figure (page 50) has two weights on the ends of a rod issuing from his shoulders. All balancing toys need to rock back and forth on a blunt strip or point (see illustrations).

Almost any shape can be made to balance if the basic rules are followed; perhaps the easiest to make for the novice toy maker is the **Balancing Parrot**. Mark out the profile, similar to the one

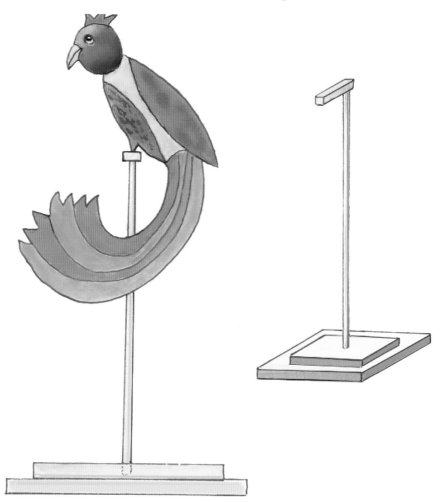

A typical (easy to make) balancing parrot and perch detail.

Toys that balance, teetering on the edge of a table or specially made stand, have continued to fascinate all age groups since they first appeared in ancient times. The exact country of origin is not recorded, but Persia is named in some sources. In England in the late eighteenth and early nineteenth centuries sets of balancing horses were used as a pub gambling game: the first horse to stop rocking was deemed to be the winner. The Victorians loved novelties that demonstrated scientific principles and the balancing toy in its many forms was a great favourite.

A stylised balancing horse from Eastern Europe circa 1930, note the loose limbs.

pictured, ensuring that the tail end is significantly heavier than the head end. My design is unique in that it doesn't only balance on its pointed foot but the beak and the first three tail feathers are also balancing points, and it will also balance face down across the perch. A true five-point balancer. The stands or supports for balancing toys can be made in more than one way. The simplest would be in the form of a short horizontal bar (perch) glued to the top of length of dowel which is in turn glued into a substantial base block. A tall, goalpost arrangement made up of two upright dowels with a short crossbar

A whole variety of materials can be used as effective weights, from modern lead-free fishing weights, to stock hardwood balls or wheels. Perhaps the easiest are just offcuts of heavy hardwood; these can look very effective if painted to look like suitcases held by a balancing figure. I have made many balancers for customers on commission - a surfer counterbalanced by a shark, a Porsche car with a real Porsche radiator badge as a weight, and so on. Another two-weight balancer in my collection was made from scrap material in a wartime shadow factory, evidence of one worker's determination to give a present during a time of great shortages.

joining them at the top makes an excellent support for the horses, especially as it looks like a horse jump. Many old balancing toys used cast lead for weights; this would not be allowed today because lead is a poisonous metal.

The two-weight balancer, if made to look like a circus performer, can be turned into a Rope Runner or Rope Rider. Fixing a basic grooved pulley wheel between the figure's feet will enable him to balance on a cord that is tightly stretched between two anchor points. Lots of fun can be had racing two or more in competition. Many clubs in the USA do just that.

The Sawyer and Workman balancers show alternative ways that a single weight can be made

An unusual balancer using a pebble as a weight.

Left: A traditional balancing sawyer from Germany.

Right: The intriguing Sky-Hook' belt balancer (amaze your friends).

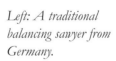

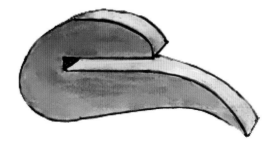

to work. One of the strangest balancing novelties is known as the **Sky-Hook**, made from hardwood. Just cut out to the profile shown in the illustration. To amaze onlookers place a trouser belt centrally into the slot, then put the point of the sky-hook on to an outstretched fingertip: the hook and belt will balance as if by magic. The simple two-weight balancer from

Balancing Toys

*Left: The wonderful
rope-rider, just
watch him go!*

*Right: A typical two
weight balancer
and stand.*

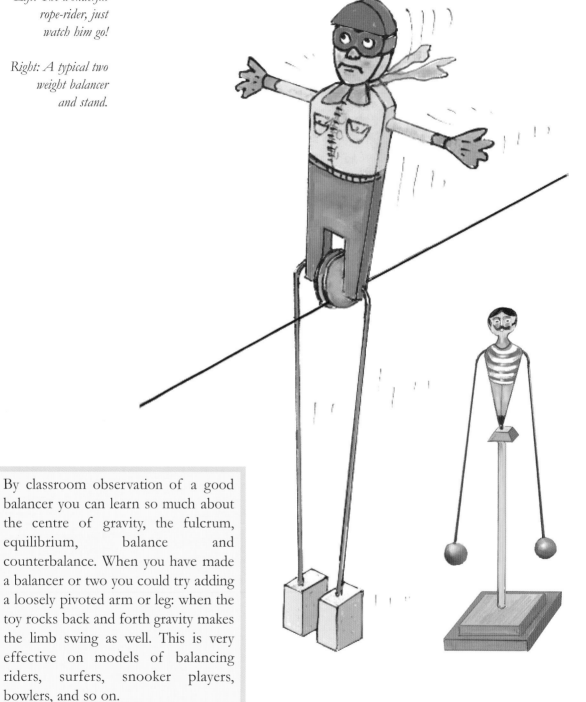

By classroom observation of a good balancer you can learn so much about the centre of gravity, the fulcrum, equilibrium, balance and counterbalance. When you have made a balancer or two you could try adding a loosely pivoted arm or leg: when the toy rocks back and forth gravity makes the limb swing as well. This is very effective on models of balancing riders, surfers, snooker players, bowlers, and so on.

50

China (illustrated) is one that can be copied easily in the classroom. The whole thing can be made from a strip of stiff card and lumps of modelling clay. To add to the fun a cut-out figure could be glued at the central point.

This two weight balancer, is very easy to make by children using found materials.

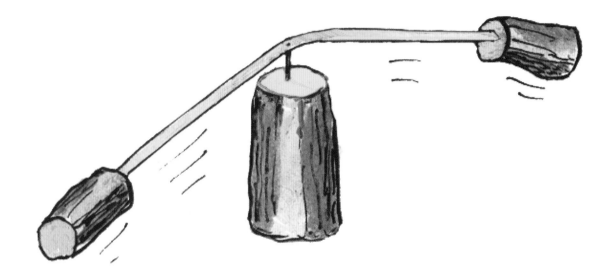

Climbing Toys

A fully assembled climbing toy, note angled holes through hands.

Double cord climbers

By drilling holes at an angle or by the judicious use of elastic bands, certain wooden toys can be made to climb up single or double cords. You will notice that the two holes in the hands need to be drilled at an angle, tipping in towards the top. The toy has a top bar or decorated top, having three holes, two for the cords and the centre hole as a pivot. The centre loop or hole needs to be fitted over a hook or screw securely fixed to a wall or door; the bar must pivot if the toy is to work. When the cords are taut and then pulled alternately, the angle creates enough friction to lift the toy on that side and so on until the toy reaches the top. Releasing both cords removes the friction, thereby allowing the force of gravity to take over, and the toy descends rapidly.

The illustrations show clearly how to make a variety of attractive two-cord climbing toys, the most basic being the wooden cut-outs with outspread limbs. You will notice that all of them have the angled holes drilled through the edge of oversized hands. Please note also that the top bar up to which the toy climbs requires three holes, one at each end and one in the middle; the cords are threaded as shown and the toy hangs from the central loop. For the more decorated tops that relate to the toy beneath, the cords are tied off at the back and a centrally placed hole becomes the pivot point. The length of the

Almost any shape can be made to climb, note the wooden carrier behind the soft mouse and the appropriate swivel tops.

cords must be appropriate to the proportions of the toy; I find that 1.5m-2m is plenty. Two wooden beads tied to the ends will prevent the toy from sliding off.

Probably the most popular figure is that of a sailor, but a little thought will bring to mind other people and professions that climb: mountaineers, rock climbers, chimney sweeps, steeplejacks, soldiers, and so on. Very young children can be highly amused by my nursery rhyme climbers. They consist of a soft-toy

Hickory Dickory Dock and **Incy Wincy Spider** can be wonderful motivators in nursery or reception classes: they not only bring the popular nursery rhymes to life, but they help to develop basic hand-eye coordination and multi-tasking.

A close up of a climbing figure. Make yours look totally different.

spider or mouse that is glued securely to a shallow U-shaped wooden carrier that also has the angled holes in the appropriate place. The basic carrier could also be glued to the back of cut-outs of hot air balloons, aircraft or even a space shuttle or rocket.

The simplest climbers have just a plain wooden bar to reach; to make the toy more attractive devise an appropriately decorated top pivot. My illustration shows a monkey climbing up to a tree; allow your imagination to rove, allowing creative ideas to flow. Now you can fit a planet above a space rocket, and so on. These toys can be cut out from any wooden board, but 12mm-15mm ply is best; MDF will work for a time but it tends to split if drilled through the edges. If cutting the profiles from a board be aware of grain direction and avoid short grain at critical points; hardwood is strongest.

Single cord climbers

The monkey or sailor relies on the friction and the stretching energy of elastic bands to give it the ability to climb a single cord in a series of jerky movements. The toy consists of a sideways-facing profile of a monkey or sailor having a pair of loosely pivoting legs and a pair of fixed arms pointing forwards. You will need to study the drawings to work out how the elastic bands work together to make the toy climb. Many old illustrations show a child with one foot through a loop at the bottom end of the cord while the other end is being jerked with a hand, thereby making the figure climb. After the toy has reached the top it needs to be pulled to the bottom again for a repeat performance. I have a heavy card version of the toy in my collection, a Second World War sailor made in the USA; the pivots are standard paper fasteners and it is rather delicate, but it still works. The toy is an excellent way to demonstrate how a pulling force plus friction, levers, pivots and

The origins of climbing toys have been lost but I suspect that the hauling of ropes and the setting of sails on old-time ships and boats have something to do with their development. While off duty on long voyages many sailors had ample time (and ability) to whittle wood, carve and paint small items as gifts for loved ones left behind. The very basic two-hole mechanism would enable a flag or sail to be hoisted to the top of a mast in the absence of a pulley wheel, and these wonderful toys follow the same principles.

These toys became very popular in the late nineteenth century, and then again during the 1930s after being featured in many children's encyclopedias, DIY books and popular magazines.

A climbing sailor with a single cord and elastic band action, N.B.the arm elastic only just grips the cord,

stretched/twisted elastic bands can make a toy work.

Push-Pull Toys on Sticks

People have been making a wide variety of animated, push-pull wooden toys for at least four hundred years. The pushing and pulling on the one or two sticks attached to the pivoted limbs or parts force the toy to move back and forth, or up and down, in a very entertaining way.

The figure of a monkey was a great favourite, but deer, dogs, cats and other animals featured strongly. You will see from the illustrations that all the animals have pivoting limbs. The two sticks have holes at the top to take wire rivets; the front limbs attach to the long stick and the hind legs to the shorter one. There are two ways to enable the short stick to slide up and down the other. First, the traditional method. You will need to use sticks of elder, cut from a hedgerow. Elder sticks have a soft, pithy centre that can be pushed out easily with another thinner stick; you will require a sharp penknife to whittle the short stick so that one end is left whole tapering up to form a single solid stick at the other (see illustration). Use a thin stick to push out the soft pith at the bottom end: it is through this that the

Among the first such toys were the animals and figures attached to the top of two sticks, made by professional toy makers across Europe, particularly in Germany. Many old engravings and pictures depict them being sold at fairs and markets, or by the travelling pedlar from his huge pack.

Left: A bear on a stick lever toy, experiment with other animals and figures, they could be made from suitable card.
Right: A loosely jointed cat mounted upon a single stick, a shaker toy.

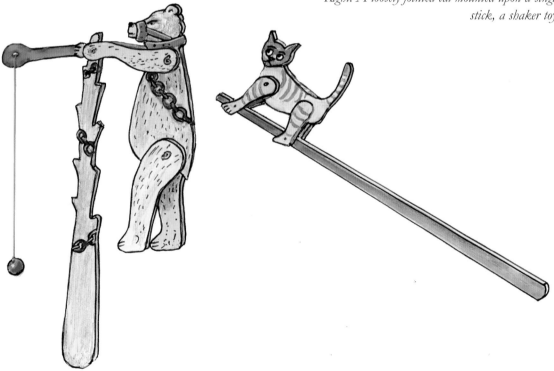

Alternative ways of constructing animated animals on sticks.

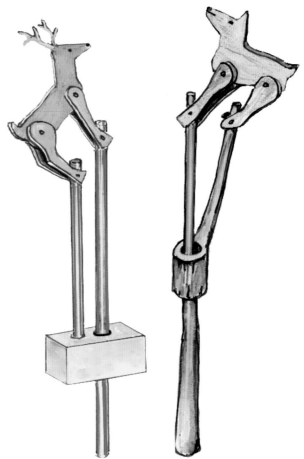

A push pull action animated butterfly, try making a bird or a flying dinosaur.

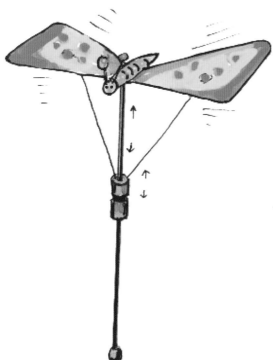

longer thinner stick is pushed and pulled to make the toy work.

The next method suits modern stock dowelling (available from most DIY outlets); 6mm and 9mm diameter rod works well. Look closely at the illustrations: you will see that the short rod is glued into a suitable block of wood, which has another hole drilled through to allow the longer (thinner) dowel to slide through. The holes in the block must be drilled close together (always use a drill vice for safety) to enable the toy to work properly. As with all folk toys, making a prototype and a little experimentation will help to create a finished toy that works smoothly and efficiently. Attach the monkey or other animal to the sticks, as shown, using wire rivets. When the sticks are pushed and pulled the animal will perform a variety of amusing acrobatics. The two-stick mechanism can also be used to make two figures turn back and forth horizontally. Look at the illustration showing two ladies holding tennis bats (page 63) and you will understand what I mean.

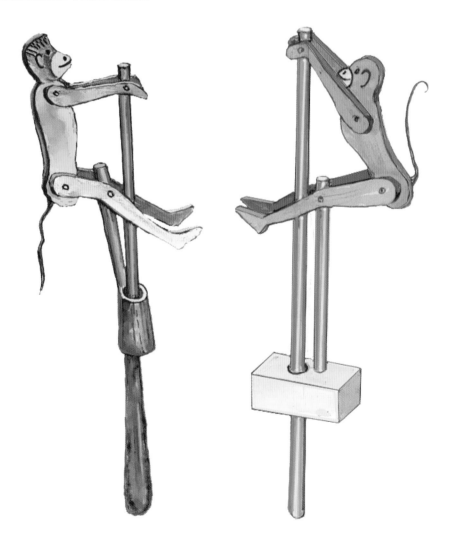

The very Victorian monkey-up-a-stick, note old and new methods of construction.

A boy playing with his monkey-up-a-stick.

The Monkey up a Stick became a great favourite in the late nineteenth and early twentieth centuries; in fact, it is mentioned in many amusing rhymes, songs and ditties. For example:

There's a drum for little Dick and a monkey up a stick,
For Sally a skipping rope and ball,
And for little Mary Lou there's a cock-a-doodle-doo,
And a rattle for our darling little baby.

*　*　*　*　*　*

When mother went to Blackpool on the Saturday morning train
She said "Now be good girls and boys till I come back again,
Be kind to little baby, and to little brother Mick,
When I come back, I'll fetch you all a monkey up a stick."
Chorus:
Mickey Mickey Mick up a sticky sticky stick
Goes clickey clickey click; eyeyooooo! eyeyooooo!
Mickey Mickey Mick up a sticky sticky stick
Is the finest little play toy that I know.'

The toy became almost as popular as Mickey Mouse between 1900 and 1914, a book entitled The Adventures of a Monkey up a Stick was published around 1900, and a music hall song about the toy was written in 1901. However, the mainly German-made toys became less popular after the First World War began and the commercially made ones faded into obscurity. Many were made by amateur craftspeople in the period between the wars, especially during the Depression.

The Bear and Blacksmith

The Bear and Blacksmith and similar toys seem to have their origins in Russian folklore, the bear being a fairly common sight in Russia's dark, snow-clad forests and mountains. The mechanism is simple, consisting of two usually flat sticks placed one above the other or side by side (see illustrations). The figures, usually two facing, can be cut out as simple flat profiles that attach on the front of the operating sticks. If you want to be a little more adventurous you could cut the figures from thicker material and fit them over the sticks by cutting suitable slots. Rudimentary chip carving will enhance your figures further; in both cases a touch of paint also helps. The variety of toys that can be made in this way is almost endless: they do not have to represent the Bear and Blacksmith figures. The

The wonderful bear and blacksmith toy from Russia, note the push-pull action, easy to make from suitable card too.

A push pull action toy like those made in 19th Century Germany.

The story of The Bear and the Blacksmith
(based on a Russian folk tale):

A blacksmith lived on the edge of a dark, cold forest in Russia. He always needed plenty of firewood to keep his forge operating. One day when he was busy collecting firewood and logs, a great black bear rushed out of the trees, roaring: 'No one is allowed to take wood from my forest.' The blacksmith was startled, but very brave; he just knew that he had to challenge the bear. 'I am only collecting firewood for my forge,' he replied. The bear roared on hearing this: 'If I catch you here again I WILL EAT YOU!' he bellowed. 'Oh! That isn't fair,' said the blacksmith. 'I am doing you no harm.' Once again, the even angrier bear roared: 'I WILL EAT YOU!' The blacksmith knew then that he was in serious danger. Then he had a wonderful idea.

He stood up to his full height and challenged the bear to a hammering contest, the winner of which would be left in peace. To his great surprise (and relief) the bear agreed. The blacksmith found a fallen tree on which they could both stand facing one another; he gave the bear his spare hammer from his tool bag. At the count of three, the contest began … WHAM! BANG! WHAM! BANG! CRASH! WHAM! BANG! … The forest echoed to the sound as the hammers moved faster and faster. Eventually, both became very tired and the hammering stopped. It was a draw: no one had won, so the bear and the blacksmith shook hands and agreed that they would share the forest for ever.

Moral of the story: rather than argue and fight over something, it is better by far to agree to share.

two operating sticks can be made to work flat side down so that the toys semi-rotate as the sticks are pushed and pulled. Note that the pairs of sticks are always placed a little way in from each other so that the opposing ends can be gripped easily.

The push pull action for these ladies lays flat making them semi rotate in an amusing manner.

Push pull fighting knights from a medieval print.

Windmills and Whirligigs

By the mid-thirteenth century the windmill on the hill became a familiar sight all over Europe. In Britain, most places had a massive timber post mill to complement the older technology of the water mill. Both were used not only to grind grain but eventually to power machines that made life easier than having to use hand tools. No one knows when and where the toy windmill was invented and first used, but toy makers came up with many variations. Among the first recorded are those depicted in early medieval woodcuts, showing, for example, two children charging towards each other with a whirling windmill revolving on the end of a long stick. This demonstrates again how far wooden toys reflected the adult world: the real joust would have been a familiar and exciting spectacle in those times, and fairs and markets surrounding any public event or religious holiday would have had stalls that sold cheap toys. This particular model, known as the Jousting Mill or Stick Mill, remained popular right up to the late nineteenth century. Another wooden creation, the Hobby-Horse or Stick-Horse, also features strongly in history; many engravings and paintings depict the stick mill and the hobby-horse being used together. The addition of an inflated pig's bladder tied with a cord to the windmill stick added to the fun - it would make an exciting drumming hoof noise as the children ran about.

Below: Boys with hobby horse, and a windmill.

Right: Medieval stick or jousting mills, the pigs bladder would make a noise like a galloping horse

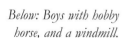

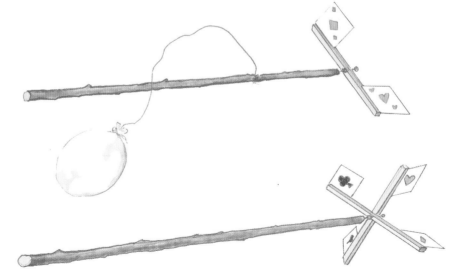

Working windmills (real or toy) are made to work by ensuring that the flat vanes or blades are set with opposing twists (see illustrations). Toy versions had very thin wooden vanes split from a board; others used goose or swan feathers. The Brueghel painting, *Children's Games*, shows that old playing cards were also used. Early jousting mills had just two vanes glued into slots, or on to the face of each end of a short stick. I have made many of these in various sizes and found that they are extremely efficient. You can make the four-vane version by creating a cross of two short sticks, achieved by cutting a halving joint at the centres. You can use the wooden cross with

A medieval boy charging with his jousting mill.

Typical toy windmills: L. 16th Century, R. 18th Century.

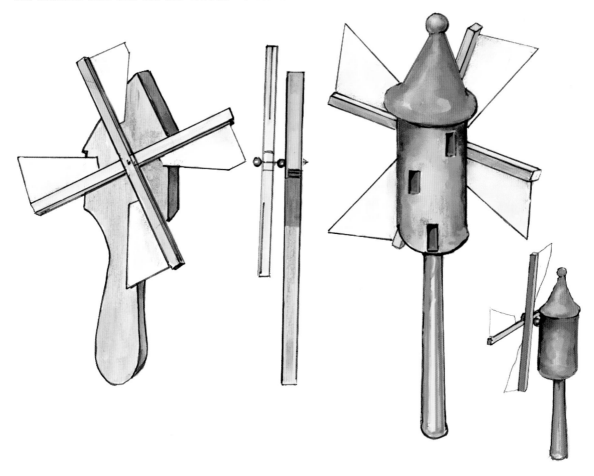

*'Children's Games'
by Flemish painter
Pieter Brughel, how
many toys and
games can you
count?
Pieter Brueghel the
Elder (c.1525 -
1569).*

Above: 18th Century street vendor selling windmills.

Right: The two ways of making paper or card windmills. Left. WWII playing card mill. Right This type remains a great favourite today.

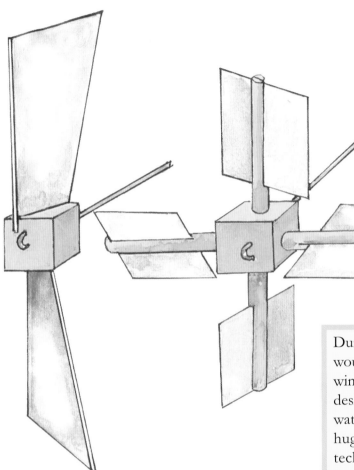

Details of windmill vane construction.

its four twisted vanes with a suitable hole drilled through the centre for many models. To make one, first cut all the sticks to size, for a standard toy about 120mm long with a 9mm square section. An easy way to cut the halving joint is to use a standard 9mm spur-point wood drill. Mark the centre point of both sticks and drill halfway through each one. You will not need to clean up the tiny rounded corners left by the drill: they help the joint to grip very firmly when they are glued and tapped together on assembly. Allow the glue to dry overnight, clean up the assembly

During the eighteenth century, pedlars would roam the streets with dozens of windmills whirling round on a specially designed frame. The invention of the water mill and the windmill led to a huge and significant step in technology. The enormous rotary force of the main axle was transmitted via a mixture of pulleys, gears, cranks and levers to a whole variety of different machinery, depending on the requirements of the owner. For example, the rotary force could be transmitted to powerful forging hammers, or other manufacturing machinery that saved hours of backbreaking work. In the Low Countries and in the English fens wind power drained the excess water from rich farmland.

The working windmill is ideal for the study of forces, mechanisms, and model making; even the simple paper/card mill on a stick can be made to make a noise. The four-vane wooden version made in a size to suit is powerful enough to drive a whole variety of models. Again, I recommend buying the appropriate books featuring working mechanisms. Remember: no batteries required.

A typical whirligig horse, very popular 'Folk Art' from the USA.

with sandpaper and then drill a centre hole that is large enough to spin on a suitable nail, panel pin or wire axle.

The easiest way to fit the four-card vanes is to stick them on to the top face of each end of the cross as it lies on the bench; after the glue is dry bend each one upwards at the same angle of 30-45 degrees. If you want to use the slot method you will need to tilt the table of your scroll saw or place a block under one end of a temporary wooden table. Hold the wooden cross very firmly (fingers away from the blade) and feed one of the ends in to cut an angled slot around 40mm long. Then cut the remaining three slots in exactly the same way, ensuring that you hold the cross the same way up for each operation. The card vanes (cut square or as blunt triangles) can be slotted and glued into place. If using the triangles the widest end is the top of the vane.

The more familiar handheld toy windmill appeared at a later period than jousting mills, and was modelled on the familiar post mill, shaped by an axe from a thin (split) oak board - but any other local timber could be used. You could try doing this if you wanted an authentic, historically accurate model. A scroll saw will make short work of cutting a quantity from 30mm-40mm pine boards; use a profile similar to the one in the illustration. All the windmills featured here will require beads or short lengths of drinking straw as spacers on the axle.

Windmill vanes can be used to power many toys or working models. Many of the early settlers in the USA originated from toy-making centres in Germany, and numerous farms and homesteads there featured a Whirligig - perhaps a model of a sailor with whirling windmill arms, or a lady frantically churning butter or washing clothes. Some were created purely for decoration; others featured clickers or bells to scare birds from crops, or they formed amusing but accurate weather vanes. A strong but simple arrangement of cranks and levers was used to create a whole variety of movements. A few ideas can be gleaned from my illustrations; should you want more I recommend that you buy an instruction book that specialises in the subject. Many old American whirligigs are highly valued as folk art today, and are worth a great deal of money. My illustration depicts a sailor whirligig figure similar to those found in many folk art collections. You can make any figure, such as a soldier with signal flags, a fishmonger with fish or even a Native American Indian paddling his canoe. All are guaranteed to work if the axle turns freely and the twist on the propeller arms is set correctly. I also show how other kinds of whirligig sails can be constructed.

Toy windmills feature strongly in China, Japan and India, in paper or card, the classic star shape formed from bent card being the most familiar. Many of these very colourful toys have tiny clickers or bells that are struck in turn by the whirling vanes. Made mainly from thin plastic today, they remain a great favourite of children everywhere. In Portugal and Spain many old windmills use cloth sails, which can be furled like those on a sailing ship; toy versions are available. All of these need a wooden stick and a nail or wire axle on which to revolve.

A whirligig sailor figure like the one in the 'Compton Verney' Folk Art collection. Experiment with other figures.

During the Second World War, when materials for manufactured toys were in short supply, we children would use an old playing card to cut out the shallow H shape shown in the illustration. A quick twist, then a pin or nail through the centre into the end of a hedgerow stick would give us an amazingly efficient windmill. However, to our fertile imaginations they became the whirling propellers of our very own Spitfire or Lancaster Bomber planes. To run around with one in each hand (or if you were lucky enough to own a bike, fixed to the handlebars) was exciting stuff. What an amazing throwback to those medieval boys running around imitating their knights in shining armour. A clear illustration of how simple toys resurface in times of hardship.

Catch Toys

Games and toys that improve users' hand-eye coordination remain just as popular today, and the simple catch toy is still a great favourite. Its origins are unknown but variations have been faithfully recorded over the centuries in many different cultures. The basic idea seems to have developed independently in many parts of the world. Good hand-eye coordination was an essential skill required by our hunting ancestors, because no kill meant little to eat, and hunger is a very powerful motivator. The native American Indian and his Eskimo neighbours developed very similar toys, consisting of a tapering stick of bone, ivory or wood having a cord or sinew tied through a hole at the thin end, then a ring and a fish shape (with a large hole) cut from hide tied to the other. A large marrow-bone was cut into five or six naturally hollow sections; more leather fish could also be made. The game was taken very seriously and was played by all ages, with adults sometimes gambling on the results.

To make the **Eskimo catch toy** using my illustration as a guide, fashion a tapered stick from any suitable wood. Make a template for the fish shape from thin card and use the template to draw a set of fish on to thin ply, fake hide or real leather. When done, cut or drill a 30mm hole through each one. To make the rings, use 15mm ply or MDF, draw them freehand or make a template, then drill the 30mm hole in each before cutting them out on the scroll saw. To play, hold the stick in one hand and the ringed end of the cord in the other, and throw each ring or fish into the air in turn while trying to catch it on the tapered stick as it falls. Work out your own points system for fish or rings caught; invent a team game.

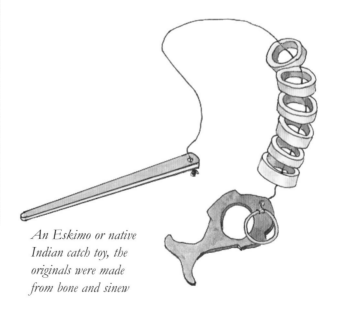

An Eskimo or native Indian catch toy, the originals were made from bone and sinew

72

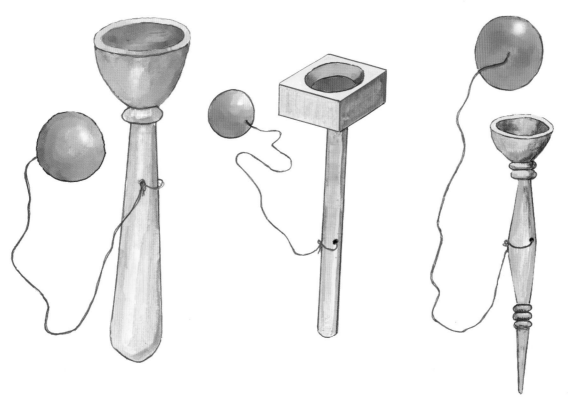

Three alternative ways to make a ball & cup catch toy, children can make a paper cone or use a plastic cup instead.

The native names for the toy included Pommawonga, Gazinta and Zimba, but more common names are **Spear the Fish**, **Hoop and Pole**, **Ring and Ping**, and the **Lovers Game**. In Europe a similar game developed, consisting of a lathe-turned wooden handle having a turned cup on the end and a ball. At first it was a fairly large, easy-to-play game enjoyed by both adults and children; then the toy grew in popularity and became smaller and much more refined, especially in the sixteenth-century court of King Henry III of France. Princes, princesses and courtiers became smitten by the craze, so much so that Henry actually banned it from his palaces as a complete time-waster. In the early eighteenth century the refined version became known as the Bilboquet; this was made from a finely turned spindle of ivory, bone, mahogany or other hardwood, and had a shallow cup at one end and a long blunt point at the other. On the end of the cord was an extra-large wood or ivory ball that had a hole drilled opposite to where the cord was fixed. Playing this game was even more difficult: the ball had to be caught both in the small shallow cup and on the blunt spike.

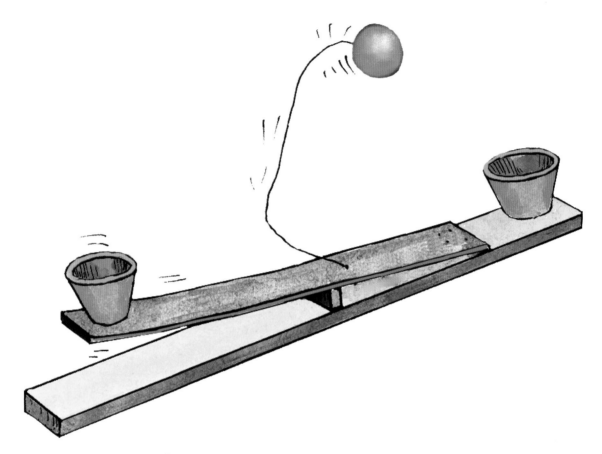

A spring board catch toy from Spain.

Turning a **cup-and-ball** on a lathe is not difficult but I recommend that a beginner take lessons in turning first; many experienced turners offer practical courses. Another way to learn is through joining a local wood-turning organization, where experienced members help newcomers. If you do not own a lathe a simple but effective cup-and-ball can be made up from offcuts. First cut a cube of wood, then mark the centre on opposite sides. Then in one side use a 25mm flat bit or forstner bit to drill a hole halfway through, then a 9mm-12mm hole from the other side. Cut a suitable length of dowel to fit into the small hole, and through this at the centre drill a 4mm hole. Sand all the parts smooth, bevelling or rounding the corners of the cube. To assemble, just glue the dowel into the block and then tie about 60cm of thin cord through the dowel. You can buy a stock 25mm wooden ball or you can shape one roughly (it doesn't need to be perfect) on a sanding belt or disc from a scrap of timber.

There is more to the game of cup-and-ball than most people think; most attempt to catch the ball by swinging it forwards and upwards, and with practice this does work. Try these methods in turn: first (by far the easiest) let the ball hang straight down under the toy and twist the cord so that the ball spins; now in one movement propel the ball straight upwards by a jerk of the hand and as it falls back catch it in the waiting cup. This is also how you can catch the ball on the spike of the Bilboquet. When you have scored a high success rate by that method you can try catching the ball by swinging it out front, then to the left, to the right and from behind in turn. A group of players can have great fun devising point-scoring or forfeits games.

It is very easy to make the flat, cut-out catch toys in the shape of a fish or clown, as shown in the illustrations. Of course, you can devise your own designs. The South American Perinola is similar to the cup-and-ball, except that instead of trying to catch a ball in a cup the player attempts to catch a heavy, lathe-turned hat shape on a blunt point. Apparently, Perinola is still a great favourite among adults in Peru. (You can buy wooden balls of all diameters from the mail-order catalogues of most craft suppliers, or by searching through the advertisements in relevant magazines.)

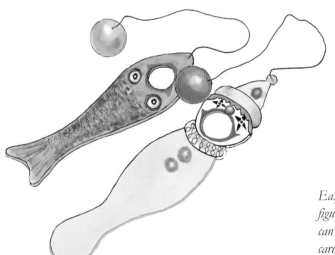

Easy to make flat-figure catch toys that can also be made from card.

Wooden Dolls

The crude - then later more refined - wooden doll has been around as long as we have. The first wooden dolls were fashioned from a bundle of twigs, or an upside down forked stick with another stick tied across for arms. A few deft cuts with a sharp edge would soon delineate facial features, and the addition of long shavings, moss or rags made hair and rudimentary clothing. Every ancient tribe and race seems to have devised its own unique version, and many were never meant as toys but for worship, or even as props during fetish and witchcraft ceremonies. Others were given to young women as fertility symbols, later given to their children as playthings, and so were among the earliest wooden toys.

Around 2000 BC the Egyptians made **Paddle Dolls**: front-facing, female figures cut out of flat boards, with stylized painted clothing, inset bead eyes and long tresses of beaded hair. Also illustrated are two Egyptian dolls that have arms that pivot at the shoulder. Many good examples still exist in specialist museum collections today.

There is an ongoing scholarly debate about what they were made and used for.

Were they intended as grave goods made as wooden slaves and concubines to accompany a dead master or mistress to the afterlife? Or maybe they were fertility symbols: quite a few examples have clearly defined pubic areas. Whatever they were meant to be, they were an ideal size for a young child's hands, and it is thought that many were used as playthings.

The pictures on this page show a few of the earliest forms of the wooden doll.

The Egyptians also devised a number of the world's first animated toys operated by pulling a cord (see illustrations). Throughout Africa crude wooden dolls have always featured strongly in tribal life, again as fertility and fetish symbols as well as children's playthings. Like toy weapons or tools, toy dolls were considered important teaching tools: with a doll a young girl would imitate the nursing, caring and homecare skills of her mother, essential for the survival of family and tribe. In Europe since the Dark Ages children have known and loved wooden dolls, some finely carved, others crudely chopped out with an axe and knife. Until the eighteenth century most were stump figures without jointed limbs, acquired at fairs or markets. There are two lathe-turned **Bartholomew Babies** preserved in the Tudor/Stuart department of the Museum of London made from English oak. The annual Bartholomew Fair was held in London from medieval times until the nineteenth century, and it was a great source of entertainment and goods of all kinds, including wooden toys. The carved oak Puritan doll at prayer is typical of many that were made as one-off items.

A Stuart stump doll or baby (Ref: Museum of London Tudor Stuart Department).

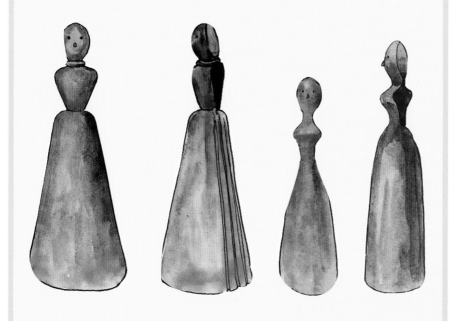

Tudor 'Bartholomew Babies' or stump dolls. Ref: Museum of London Tudor/Stuart department.

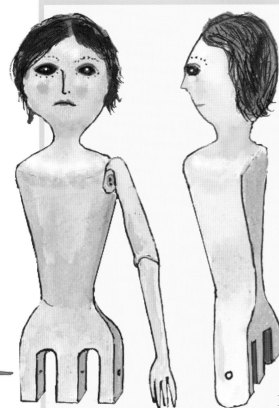

The word 'doll' did not actually surface until the mid-eighteenth century: before this they were always referred to as 'babies'. In the early eighteenth century, society in general became more refined, and woodworking and craft skills improved, all to be reflected in the types of wooden toys and dolls available. Huge changes in fashion brought about the existence of large fashion dolls, beautifully turned and carved figures stylishly dressed. Grand ladies across Europe and even in the New World would rush to see the latest French creations, modelled in miniature as soon as the ship carrying them docked. During the Napoleonic Wars of the early nineteenth century the fashion dolls and escorts even had special passports to ensure their continued safe passage: pampered women could not go without their fine clothes and dolls.

A typical 18th Century doll with human hair, pupil-less brown glass eyes and kid-leather arms.

As the century wore on, English dolls for children reflected the grander fashion dolls: they were lathe-turned in fruitwood, had beautifully carved and painted features, real human hair that was nailed on under a bonnet, and pupil-less dark brown, glass eyes that seemed to stare straight at the onlooker. They too wore hand-stitched dresses and petticoats reflecting fashions of the day. Numerous contemporary paintings and engravings depict little girls clutching or even mistreating their dolly. One story tells of how an unfortunate doll ended up lost on the nursery fire and one of my line illustrations depicts two infants arguing over a large wooden doll. When Queen Victoria was a little girl she amassed a large collection of beautifully made **Peg Woodens**, dolls that had painted and carved features and fully articulated wooden limbs. The young princess Victoria dressed and named each one, and her collection still exists today in the Victoria and Albert Museum in London.

A pair of stylised stump dolls from Eastern Europe or Germany 19th Century

From the late eighteenth century right up to 1914, almost every wooden toy available in the toyshops of Europe and America was of German origin. The coming of mail-order catalogues and vast improvements in transport increased the demand for cheap, mass-produced toys, and the German family co-operatives that produced most of them became slicker and quicker. As a result the cruder peg wooden or **Dutch Doll** emerged. Lathe-turned quickly from pine, the backs were hastily split, and the hips and joints roughly cut, then holes were drilled at the

Above: 'Tis MY doll' an argumentative pair of girls 18th Century.
Below: The stages in the construction of a Victorian 'Peg Wooden' or 'Dutch Doll'. These were made in the millions in the Grödner Tal.

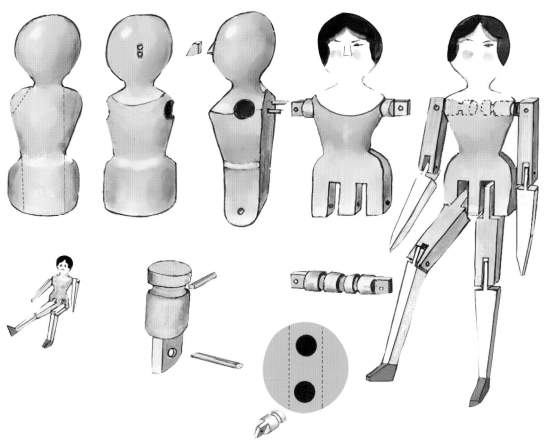

shoulders ready to receive the shoulder and arm joints. The limbs consisted of little more than chopped sticks, jointed at knees and elbows, the lower halves of which were painted white, while little red or black shoes were painted on the tiny feet. After the white paint on the head had dried, bright blue dots were added for eyes, then black pupils and eyebrows; most have fixed stares and a rather severe rosebud-red mouth. Hair was painted with a central parting; some had lighter curls painted at the forehead, and larger versions sported an inset wooden nose. They were churned out in thousands, and in England they were referred to as Dutch dolls, because they travelled from Germany via the Hook of Holland. In fact they are Deutsch dolls. They were made in sizes, from a large and heavy 60cm tall down to a tiny thing that could easily fit inside a thimble or miniature egg. Most did not survive - they were noted for breaking very easily - but many toy museums and collections contain at least one.

In the late nineteenth century the Schoenhut toy manufacturer produced beautifully carved, realistic-looking baby dolls with patented posable ball joints. All across Europe poorer children made do with the more folksy Poupard, a simple wooded stump doll painted with bright traditional designs representing the swaddling clothes worn by peasant babies. The ubiquitous German toys lost favour during the World Wars, but wounded servicemen made wooden toys as therapy during convalescence. During the First World War the British general Lord Roberts set up workshops for recovering allied service men, and they made an assortment of items that could be sold to the general public, including the attractive little posable doll illustrated here. During the 1950s Poland's traditional toy makers started to produce wooden toys again, and among the most popular were turned wooden dolls of beech wood, dressed in the typical rock-and-roll fashions of the day.

Above: A French Poupard stump doll, a very stylised baby in swaddling clothes.
Below: All round views of a little jointed doll made in the 'Lord Robert's' rehabilitation workshops set up after WWI to help the recovery of service men.

Jig Dolls or **Dancing Dolls** originated as the essential props of many itinerant street entertainers. The Jolly Boy was among the most famous; not so politically correct were the American Dancing Sambos. It seems that jig dolls first became a popular prop in street theatre during the sixteenth century, brought to England by travelling Italian musicians. They amazed audiences by demonstrating the antics of their Marionette à la Planchette, a single or pair of loose-limbed wooden dolls usually in full costume. The musician stood on one end of a plank and at the other end was fixed a turned wooden post about 60cm tall; a cord was strung from the top of this to the musician's knee, and the dolls were suspended (via holes at the

An 18th Century street entertainer with his 'Marionette's-a-la-Planchette' jig dolls .

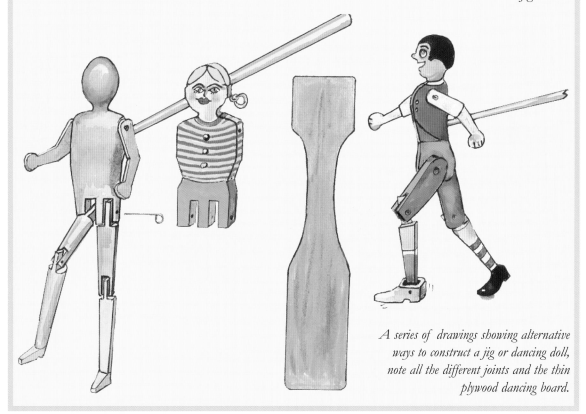

A series of drawings showing alternative ways to construct a jig or dancing doll, note all the different joints and the thin plywood dancing board.

shoulder) halfway along with their feet just touching the plank. The musician would strike up merry jigs or reels with his fiddle or fife and drum, and while beating time with his foot the cord transmitted jerky movements to the dolls. It is well recorded that onlookers were amazed and much amused by their antics. Later, the jig doll and board appeared, and right up until the 1950s travelling musicians entertained delighted audiences in pubs, in the street and at fêtes and fairs. At first the jig doll was a crude affair, carved roughly from a branch or offcut. I have an excellent example in my collection: the doll has no features, just an egg-shaped head and no arms, but it has beautifully carved and jointed legs complete with fashionable tall boots. During the Depression many unemployed miners made simple jig dolls and boards as a way of earning a few coppers in local pubs and clubs, or even on the street corner. The folk song 'Seth Davey' reflects these hard times. Clog dancing was a popular form of entertainment enjoyed by the working classes: many a half-drunk labourer, miner or bargee would willingly jump on to a pub table to demonstrate his rhythmic footwork. The Irish navvies who helped build England's network of canals and railways also brought their country's lively jigs and reels to the fore.

Dancing Bristle Dolls are strange little figures that can easily be made from short sections of broomstick dowel or even from discarded wine corks. Those illustrated are a little more complicated in that they have tiny legs dangling from a wire underneath a hollowed-out lower body. Their secret is the four stiff bristles (from a yard broom) on which they stand: just place one on top of a piano or on the top of a loudspeaker box and when music is played they jig around merrily as if by magic. They were enjoyed for many years as Christmas stocking fillers. You can still fashion a passable wooden doll from a wooden spoon or from an old-style 'dolly' clothes peg. To a child

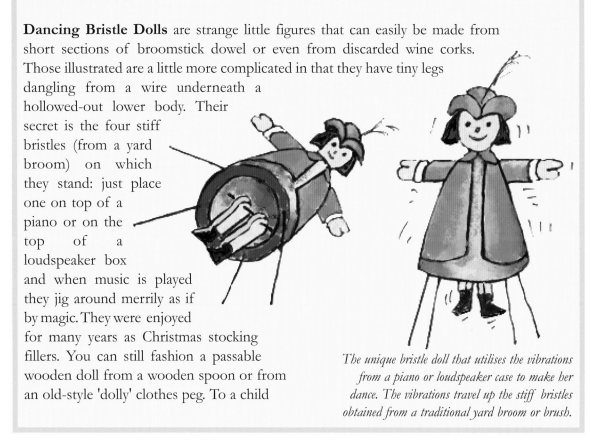

The unique bristle doll that utilises the vibrations from a piano or loudspeaker case to make her dance. The vibrations travel up the stiff bristles obtained from a traditional yard broom or brush.

that has never held a more sophisticated doll it soon becomes a favourite toy ready to share in hours of creative play. Even a dressed wooden spoon with a face and a shoebox buggy can give hours of happiness to a toddler.

I place wooden **Toy Soldiers** in the dolls section because they represent miniature human figures. Whole regiments of these extremely popular toys were available in Victorian times, almost all originating from the famous toy makers of Germany. Invariably they were lathe-turned then brightly decorated to reflect the colourful uniforms of the period. Children (especially boys) loved to line up opposing squadrons of wooden soldiers, all ready to be knocked over by the accurate rolling of a marble or a shot from a toy cannon powered by a spring or elastic band. The Brontë children in nineteenth-century Haworth (Yorkshire) made many references to their toy soldiers in their childhood journals.

Typical toy soldiers of the Victorian era, most were made in Germany. Traditionally a boys toy, they came in sets sometimes with a fort or a cannon that really fired.

Wheeled Toys (small)

Wheeled toys have a long history, the wooden horse on wheels being the all-time favourite of many cultures from ancient times onwards. Concentrating on a basic chassis on to which any superstructure/animal shape can be placed will give the maker plenty of opportunity to experiment. The simplest form of chassis has four wheels attached to a plain rectangular board. The Y-shaped chassis illustrated is much lighter and it offers more scope to the budding inventor. Because of the Y configuration it can form the basis for a three or four-wheeled vehicle, the single wheel being fitted centrally as shown. (This is an ideal project for schools, museums or for a rainy day at home.)

You can fit a whole variety of axles, such as thin dowel, bamboo skewer, coat hanger wire,

A Romano Egyptian wheeled horse, wheeled toys remain as great favourites for very young children.

discarded knitting needles, and so on. Wheels will revolve more freely and friction reduced by drilling the holes to take short sections of plastic drinking straw as bearings within which the axles revolve. For teaching purposes, a basic chassis like this can be made to move in various ways starting with the simple push or pull ideal for junior science. The force of gravity can be used to good effect: a simple adjustable ramp made from scraps or even books and card is ideal. Place the vehicle at the top then release: the distance the vehicles travel depends on the dimensions of the ramp and the friction at the axle bearings. If a thin cord tied to the front of the chassis is allowed to hang over the edge of a table the progressive addition of weights (spring clothes pegs are ideal) will eventually pull the vehicle along. Again, this clearly demonstrates gravity at work: more weight equals more speed. Next, place the ramp so that the cord falls over its highest end: pupils can then discover how many extra weights are required to overcome the changing height of the incline. Next, try using wind power: the addition of a tall mast and suitable sail will turn that basic chassis into a fine land yacht; now find out whether three or four wheels are more efficient. Then experiment: should the pair be at the front or at the rear? Will fixing the wheels further out on a longer axle increase stability?

Further power can be obtained through the use of a thin, flexible, bow-like stick fitted tightly into a hole at the opposite end to the pair of wheels. One end of a strong thread is tied through a small hole drilled through the centre of the axle, then the other end is tied to top of

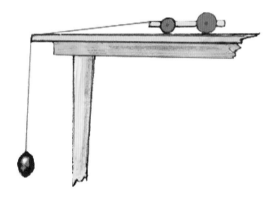

This wheeled chassis (see text) moves via the gravitational pull of the weight at the end of the cord, a great toy for experiments.

Details of my Y shaped 3 or 4 wheeled chassis, the springy stick transfers rotating motion to the axle via the strong thread, alternatively try an elastic band.

the bendy stick. As the chassis is pushed, the thread goes into tension and the stick bends like a bow. On release, the car will shoot forwards and travel a fair distance relative to tension and

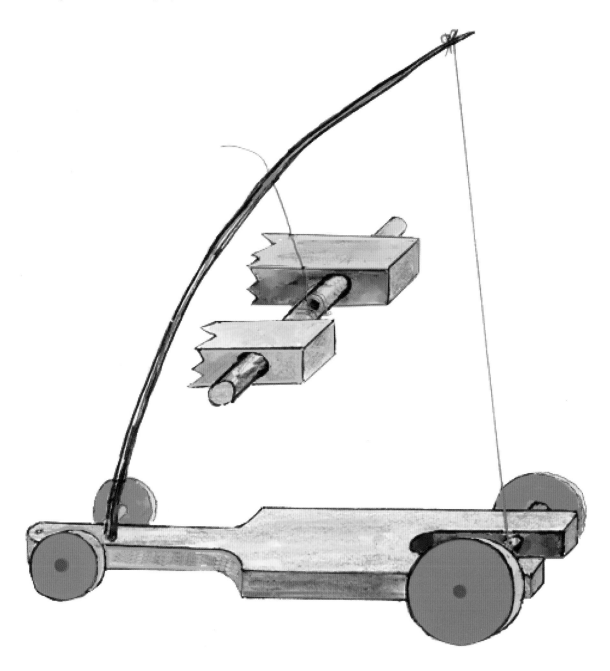

friction; also, it will automatically stop then reverse for a little way. You can experiment further with different sticks, or even coil springs fixed at one end and then by a thread to the axle. You can apply the tensioning forces of elastic band power in more than one way to make the chassis move along by hooking a small elastic band over a nail at the front end of the car and a thread going to the hole in the axle. The car will now respond in exactly the same way as in the experiment above. Even more exciting is to make an elastic band motor that is mounted on the chassis so that it turns a standard model aircraft propeller. Again, lots of experimentation is needed to work out the best ways of overcoming friction on the motor bearings created by the twisting tension of the elastic band. Short sections of drinking straw fitted into axle holes make excellent bearings; if you are able, experiment with thin metal tubing and lubricants.

The lessons learned above can now be put to good use, as we move towards using batteries together with a compatible model electric motor. By experimenting with the different ways that

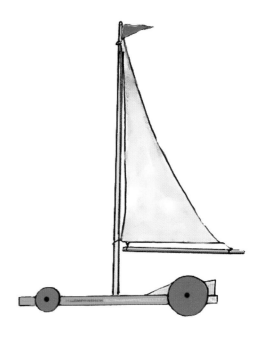

My chassis rigged as a land yacht, try galleon type sails too; experiment.

A combination of my chassis and my elastic motor, great fun!

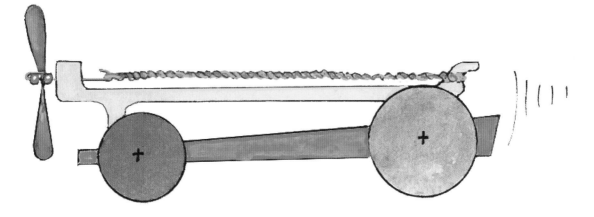

the drive can be used to power the chassis along, a great deal of fun can be had. For example, you can mount the motor sideways with the drive shaft as a friction drive to one of the wheels - a good example of where friction can be used positively. Another method of propulsion would be to mount a plastic propeller on to the drive shaft to push or pull the chassis along. You will soon learn that control (or lack of it) is an essential part of vehicle design. If you are feeling clever you may wish at this point to experiment with radio control, then go on to building more sophisticated models, from kits or from scratch. The lessons learned from building the very basic models will stand you in good stead. Remember that the same principles apply

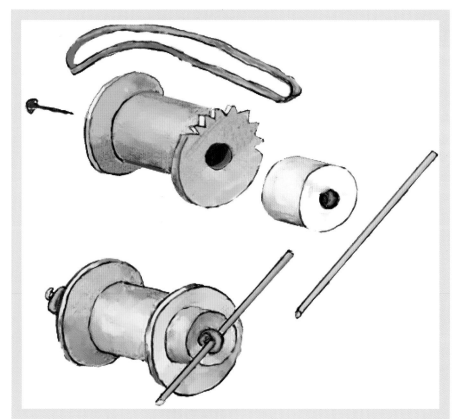

The wonderful and amazing cotton reel tank, so simple yet so powerful, if using plain dowel use elastic bands as tyres for grip.

to model boats and aircraft, except that you will need to learn more about efficient propulsion through water or the air.

When commercially made toys were almost impossible to buy during the World Wars, the **cotton reel tank** was a favourite that reflected the powerful destructive forces of the real thing. Better still, it was made from easily found materials, namely a wooden cotton reel, an elastic band, a short length of candle, a small nail and a short, thin stick. Sadly, wooden cotton reels are no longer available, but a 6cm length of broomstick or 40mm-diameter dowel will do. To make the tank, first drill a 6mm hole centrally through the length of the dowel, then carefully cut and drill a 2cm length of household candle (youngsters may need help with this). Next, hammer the nail into one end of the dowel leaving about 1cm sticking out. Look at the illustrations for reference, make an engine hook from a length of thin wire, then use it to make assembling the tank much easier. First, thread the candle on to the hook, then the cotton reel with nail at the top; hook a suitable elastic band over the nail and use the hook to pull the other end right through the dowel and the candle, then push the short thin stick through the loop, thereby keeping the elastic band in place. You should now have a tank all set to perform and amaze. Hold the tank in one hand while winding up the elastic by turning the stick: the increasing tension will pull the candle tightly into the side of the reel forming a slow-release clutch mechanism.

Now for the experiments: in its basic form the tank will happily attempt to climb up slopes and

Although not strictly a wheeled toy the **cotton reel tank** consists of a wooden roller that moves by itself as if by magic. It appeared on the scene after the First World War and became very popular again during the Second World War. This simple-to-make toy is powered by a single elastic band twisted through its hollow centre; it can crawl powerfully up a 45-degree slope and clamber over outstretched fingers or other obstacles laid in its path. If you place it underneath a suitable plastic or card container decorated to look like a robot, this old toy is brought right up to date ready for a game of Robot Wars. Place two or more wound-up models on a table top and let the wars begin; a fall off the edge, a lost engine or a complete stalemate is all part of the fun, together with marks for design and aggression.

over obstacles, but invariably it will be beaten by lack of friction - that is, no grip. Make notes on how far or high the model can climb. To discover how to improve on performance you must make slight modifications, namely tyres. With the old-style cotton reel with flanges at each end it was easy: a series of V-shaped cuts around the circumference made tank-like tracks that bit on obstacles. With the dowel model, small elastic bands round each end will make very efficient tyres, but best of all is the application of circles of latex adhesive (Copydex) allowed to dry to form a gripping surface like that on racing tyres. When the tank has tyres you will find that its efficiency is greatly improved. Have fun.

An amusing pull toy with a friction drive to the horizontal platforms from Eastern Europe.

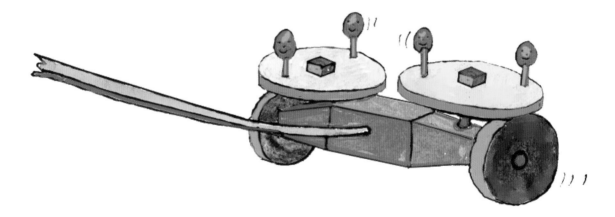

Elastic Band Power

As a result of my research into Cayley's glider (look in an encyclopedia) I came up with a simple design for a very adaptable and efficient elastic motor that can be used to power many different models. One look at the drawings should make things clear: no balsa wood is used, but ordinary pine or deal just like the model pioneers. All sizes can be made to suit any particular model: long for aircraft and shorter for powering a wheeled chassis like those described in the previous section. Start by marking out the profile on to a suitable straight-grained pine board, then use a scroll saw or fret saw to cut all the way round. Next, rip the thick profile into three or four thin ones not more that 5mm thick. Sandpaper each one until smooth, then drill a tiny hole through the front at a slight angle as shown; the downward tilt improves propeller performance for flying models. A reshaped paperclip, a couple of small beads and suitable elastic bands are all that you need to make it work.

SAFETY NOTE: A whirling propeller can be

As well as the cotton reel tank described (pages 89-90), the stored energy within a stretched or twisted elastic band can be the source of power for many other wooden toys. One of the simplest to construct is the little paddleboat seen in the illustrations: it is so simple that it needs no instructions. One of the most common applications of elastic band power is its use on model aircraft. These can be bought for very little nowadays but there is much to be gained by designing and making your own from scratch. A stock of balsa wood and an elastic motor kit from a model shop could be a starting point, but I want to encourage you to use found materials instead. My research into wooden toys of all kinds led me to study many out-of-print craft books (invariably for boys) from between 1890 and 1950. The earliest reflect the string bag aircraft of the times. Incredibly, working models kept pace with developments in the real thing. All through that period enthusiasts, young and old, were enjoying the discovery of models that really flew.

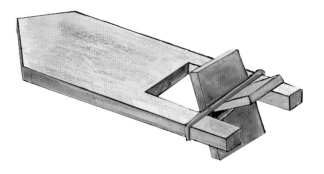

A very easy to make paddle boat with an elastic band motor.

91

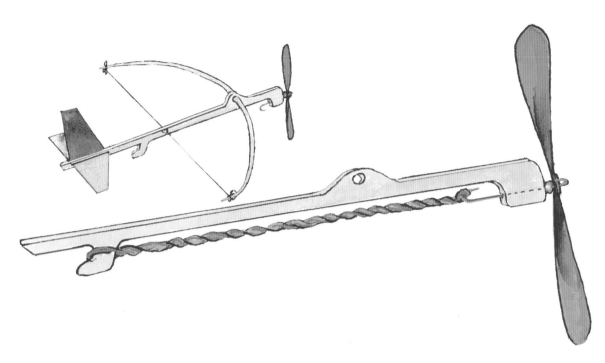

My elastic band motor adapted for flying models is based upon 'Cayley's Glider' and the earliest planes; experiment with alternative wings and rudders, etc.

dangerous; please take care to keep fingers and faces clear. The same goes for flying models: ensure that the flying area is clear of humans and animals. Be aware that stretched elastic bands can break and fly out. Remember that a propeller revolving backwards reverses its thrust, forcing the plane or toy to go backwards. Play safely at all times.

The stretching force of elastic bands can be used in many ways to make very exciting toys and games. I know that guns have a bad press nowadays but shooting at targets is a harmless and enjoyable activity that helps to develop good hand-eye coordination. I call my toy a **Target Shooter** rather than a gun, but it necessarily has to be made in the shape of a pistol. Study the drawings and you will see that you need to cut out a typical revolver shape from a board between 22mm and 30mm thick. Look closely and you will see a bump about a third of the way down the butt; it is on this that a flat wooden lever (trigger) pivots. After cutting out the shape, sandpaper it all round until smooth. Use permanent pens or acrylic paint to decorate it in bright colours or with a fantasy logo (so that it looks nothing like a real gun). The trigger is simply a flat strip of wood the same width as the stock is thick. The drawings clearly show how elastic bands are used to assemble it, some of

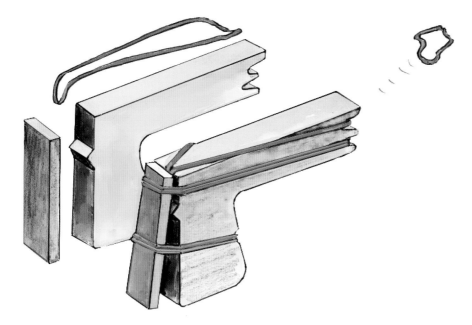

An elastic band 'Target Shooter' a Trading Standard's approved shooting toy, great fun under supervision(see text).

With a little thought and planning various methods of fixing wings, a tail and rudder will suggest themselves. One of the most exciting models in this range is the vertical take-off or high-speed type. For any model aircraft to fly it needs to be based on the principles that keep the real thing in the air. That is too much to include here so studying books on the subject will be of great help to the budding modeller. To use my universal motor on a wheeled chassis or on a working toy boat, you will need to invent ways of mounting it so that the propeller has plenty of clearance all round. You will find that experimentation of this kind is an invaluable aid to learning the basics of physical science. For lightweight toys and models I recommend the use of centre cane; it is available in a variety of diameters, from 3mm to 10mm, and you can buy it from specialist suppliers such as the Cane Store catalogue.

which are used as ammunition. Devising suitable targets can be great fun, with cans, small boxes and old CDs hanging from cords or cut-out card shapes slotted into wooden blocks.

A **cannon** that really shoots is easily made from any hollow tube such as bamboo, elder sticks, pen barrels or any thin plastic tube and scraps of wood. To make the trigger mechanism, stretch an elastic band across the lower end of the tube held in place by small nails or by another elastic

The exploding target game that uses marbles and elastic bands to shoot the trapdoors open, make a row of arches like the marbles bridge (A 1930s home-made toy).

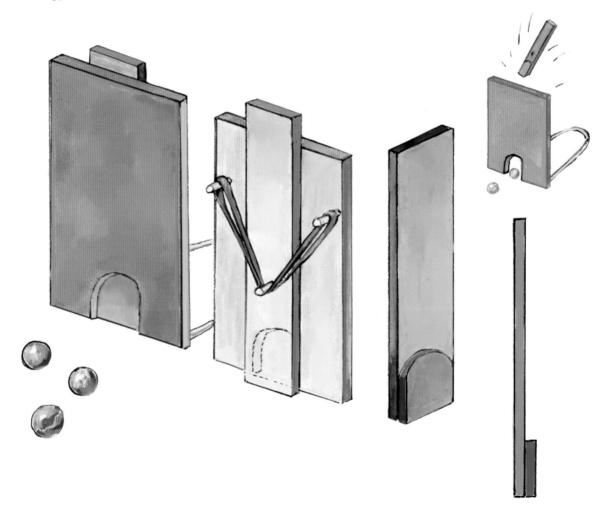

band wound tightly around the tube. A more sophisticated type incorporates a simple plunger mechanism similar to the one detailed for the Bagatelle marble launcher. I strongly recommend that the targets be placed inside a large box decorated in fairground colours: this makes easy recovery of ammunition, and elastic bands aren't left all over the place. While this type of game complies with Trading Standards regulations, strict safety rules apply at all times; elastic bands can sting so never aim them at any living thing. Adult supervision is recommended.

Another exciting and easy-to-make game is the **Exploding Target**, again using the explosive energy of a stretched elastic band. Please ensure that the tensioned elastic bands aren't too tight: a slacker tension is preferred for ease of use and for safety. You can choose to make a single-arch type incorporated into a model building or boat, or a multiple-arch bridge having the scoring figures on the target strips.

Another great favourite of toy makers is the mysterious **Hookey**, a simple, ingenious trick that will fool anyone not knowing the secret. To make a Hookey, cut a length of square stock and then shape it to a point as shown, then sandpaper it until very smooth. One third of the way along, cut off the pointed end, drill the centre to receive a length of 6mm dowel, and glue this into the hole. Cut the protruding dowel about 6mm shorter than the remaining block then carefully shape it like a hook. Use a 7mm bit to drill the block almost all the way through its length: the dowel should be a sliding fit. Glue and wedge a short length of a small elastic band into a single hole at the end opposite the point;

The Exploding Target was devised during the First and Second World Wars. I learned how to make exploding targets from an 85-year-old visitor to my crafts stall, who described in great detail how, during the Depression, he and his pals constructed them from discarded boxes; judging by the smile on his face as he spoke I could tell just what pleasure this exciting toy gave those young boys. Exploding warships targeted by elastic powered torpedoes became available during the Second World War. I remember them well: the exploding mechanism for the ships was a standard spring mousetrap - too dangerous to consider nowadays. A careful study of the illustrations will make the structure and assembly clear.

The Hookey trick, a devious way to fool your friends, easy to make and great fun.

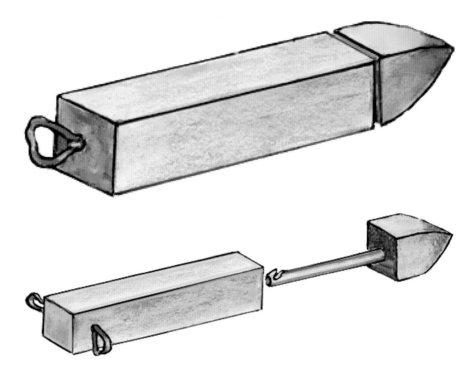

or two separate loops on either side. Either way it gives the appearance of a complete elastic band passing through or into the block. Use a wax polish to produce a shiny surface to all the wooden parts. You are now ready to fool and frustrate all and sundry. Show them how you can use the hook to catch the (non-existent) loop hidden deep inside the block. With a little manipulation, while smiling and chatting the elastic is caught, all clearly demonstrated by the forceful clicking made by the pointed block being pulled back then returned sharply. The secret (not to be told, only to be sold): the hook can never hook the non-existent elastic, but you give every indication that it is by the careful manipulation of the pointed block and dowel. Just hold the point between finger and thumb, pull gently back and squeeze: the block and dowel will shoot into the hole with a loud and satisfying click. A little showmanship and a repeat or two will convince your victim that you have succeeded. Hand the Hookey over and watch as they struggle to get that silly little hook over a non-existent elastic loop. I have witnessed grown men almost in tears begging to know the secret.

The Button in a Tin, Spider in a Packet, Rattlesnake/Scorpion in an Envelope, and so on, are all variations of the same very amusing toy. They consist of a button, or a thin, flat oval of ply, MDF or card suspended on a tightly twisted elastic band restrained from unwinding by being kept in a shallow tin, envelope or packet. During the Second World War we made our own from old tobacco tins and discarded buttons. The packet or tin should have a convincing label stating that the contents consist of a dried spider, rattlesnake eggs or any other horrible poisonous creature or insect. Instructions should also state that it should be opened slowly and with great care. When an unsuspecting victim opens the package, they will be

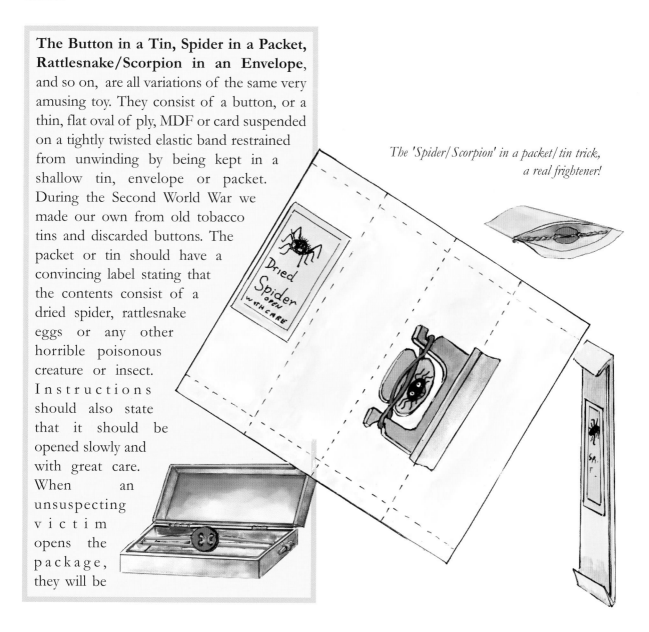

The 'Spider/Scorpion' in a packet/tin trick, a real frightener!

startled by the loud and scary noise made by the rapidly untwisting fake creature.

Jumping Frog also uses the sudden release of a twisted elastic band to surprise unsuspecting victims. All of the following variations use a sticky substance to hold temporarily the twisted elastic in check. Eventually the torsion overcomes the adhesion and the elastic unwinds with great force, thereby launching the frog high into the air. The earliest record I have of the toy comes from a late Victorian book that has an engraving showing a similar item made from the raw wishbone of a chicken. The natural springiness of the tough Y-shaped bone supplied the elastic-band-type power. A thin doubled cord was stretched between the tops of the Y forks then twisted up with a thin twig, which in turn was restrained by sticking the end into a blob of sticky beeswax, resin or tar. These toys were also known as Upjacks, and children would stand in a circle all ready to shout UPJACK! as soon as the toy jumped. The one who shouted at exactly the right time was deemed the winner.

After elastic bands were invented the ingenuity of home toy makers increased. Right up until the 1930s half a walnut shell (looks just like a baby frog) was drilled on each side to take a small elastic band, a twig lever was twisted and then the end was stuck into a blob of tar from off the side of the road. Later, transfer-printed frogs pressed from tin were widely available from toyshops, fairgrounds and street-sellers.

I invented the flat ply or MDF **Flipping Frog** some years ago, based on the research above. To make one, mark out then cut round the flattened frog shape ensuring that the hind feet form hooks for the elastic band. Sandpaper and then paint it as desired, and when dry, stretch an elastic band across the hind feet as shown. Half a lollipop stick makes an ideal lever with which to twist the elastic. Use a pea-sized lump of Blu-Tack or similar tacky stationery putty as the temporary adhesive. To make the frog jump, twist the elastic towards the frog's head about three times; you will need to pass the end of the lever past its tail to do this, by sliding it through the elastic. Carefully put the end of the tensioned lever into the Blu-Tack and press the frog firmly down. The frog will sit there grinning

Flipping Frogs, my version of a Victorian favourite (see text for details).

for a short time, then suddenly jump, startling any observers. A little adjustment of twisting or size of Blu-Tack may be needed to ensure consistent and repeated performances.

I have already explained how to make a glider or an elastic powered plane from my own design.

Two or more of these frogs can be used as part of a very amusing game that I invented myself. First, decorate a large paper plate, a thin circle of card, MDF or ply to look like a lily pond. Use a large black marker to divide the circle into quarters, then into each quarter draw wriggly tadpoles, one in the first segment, and so on. To play, place two or more ready-to-jump frogs around the pond with their feet just touching the edges. The first frog to jump scores agreed points, but points can be added for any later frog landing squarely on tadpoles. Most of the above would be ideal projects for school craft events, or as part of a business venture scheme. You will see that a simple elastic band can be the source of much fun and learning, and so much cheaper than expensive plastic toys that are discarded after a very short time.

Flying Toys

Two very similar flyers follow: they are easy to make from small scraps of wood and thin dowel or bamboo. First, the **Taketombo** (Dragonfly) of Japanese origin: it consists of a lightweight propeller mounted on the top of a thin bamboo stick. Today they are sold in little clear film packets ready to assemble, and the propeller is usually highly coloured. Next is the heavier European version of the same toy, referred to here as a **Puddle Jumper**; both seem to originate in the late eighteenth century. Both toys fly rapidly upwards, helicopter-like at great speed, and then descend rotating more slowly, very much like a sycamore seed. To fly them, place the dowel or stick between flattened palms

Two versions of the Japanese 'Taketombo' or 'Dragonfly' a great favourite with all age groups there. The larger UK versions are also known as puddle-jumpers.

with the propeller upwards. Most taketombos only work when spinning anti-clockwise, therefore it is essential that your left hand is behind your right. For safety, keep your face to one side as you quickly slide one palm over the other to set the propeller rotating; a good taketombo can rise up to ten metres before falling gracefully to earth. The heavier puddle jumper flies just as well but not so high. In late Victorian times, puddle jumper propellers were set inside a turned wooden handle very similar to those used for launcher tops (see Spinning Tops and Toys): a sharp pull of the cord and up they went. Nowadays, safer versions are available in plastic, usually with a protective guard ring around the propeller tips. For more information on flying toys I recommend that you study specialist publications then visit model shops, or even join a club. All flying toys need to be used with great care, preferably under adult supervision in a clear area.

Skittles

Skittles, Ninepins and similar knockdown games count among the earliest games recorded. Skittle-like games have a long history in Britain, played in the Middle Ages by rich men who had the luxury of a paved courtyard, or by the labouring classes wherever they could. They were even banned at various times because they were seen as a distraction for men who should have been working, or in church, or practising their archery. The game of **Klub Kayles**, also devised in medieval times, was very similar to skittles; in fact, the distinctive tapered pins were interchangeable with skittles (see drawing on next page). They could also be used either way up: the pointed ends were used in soft ground or pasture or they could be stood up on their wide bases during hard frosts or on sun-baked soil. Because the game is so old, there have been endless changes in the rules, and players adapt accordingly. Kayles and

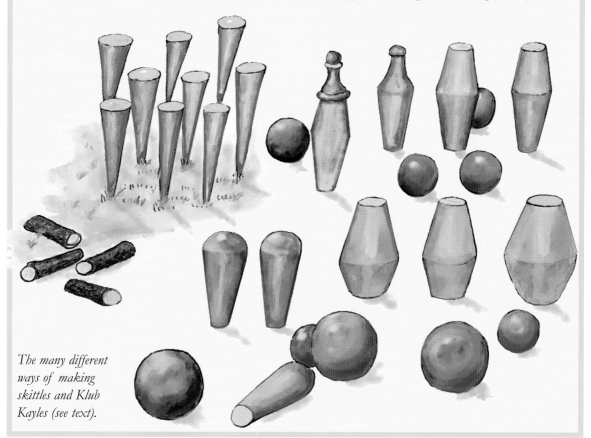

The many different ways of making skittles and Klub Kayles (see text).

skittles can be felled by throwing short clubs (klubs) or by rolling heavy wooden balls or flat wooden cheeses. Some versions of the game include taller kingpins; the way that the pins are set out can vary from place to place, sometimes in a diamond, or in a block of nine.

Today's tenpin bowling was introduced to counter a ban on ninepins. In Britain, many pubs

retain old skittle and ninepin games, some in large outbuildings (for example, in Somerset and Devon) where both the pins and the balls are large and heavy. Some pubs have a much smaller version played on leather-padded tables (in Leicestershire, for example) where short, hard sticks or round hardwood cheeses

Medieval children playing Skittles and Klub Kayles

are thrown at the tabletop pins. Other larger games might be played in a barn-like building that contains a long sloping trough for returning played balls. Bowling for a real live pig at village fêtes, fairs and carnivals was very popular up until the early 1960s. For rustic games the pins were large and heavy, turned green on a pole lathe from any suitable hardwood; the balls were turned in the same way. In Tudor and later times table-top skittles developed, and the pins became smaller and much more refined (a quick look at my drawing shows many variations). In Victorian times rows of turned and painted soldiers, or brightly painted figures decorated with alphabets and numbers, could be lined up ready to be knocked over. Another version is the well-known bar skittles: a set of pins on a board that can be felled by a ball swinging at the end of a cord swivelling from the top of a post. A related pub game common in Oxfordshire is the Aunt Sally, a single, skittle-like, turned doll mounted on a swivelling bracket that is stuck into the ground.

All of the variations described above are easy to make: if you do not own a lathe you can use sections of suitable tree branch, or cut and carve flat skittles from 40mm-60mm thick board. Throwing sticks (klubs) can be made in a similar way, or you can get stock wooden balls from crafts suppliers. As to the rules, perhaps it is best to make up your own - or you could nip down to the pub to discover what rules they play by.

Spinning Tops and Toys

The spinning top in its many forms goes a long way back in history. The Ancient Egyptians, Greeks, Romans, Chinese and Japanese - and indeed most other societies since - recorded spinning tops as favourite items both for play and learning. Scholars suggest that the earliest spinning tops may have been accidental discoveries made by idle hands - such as the spinning of a pine cone or a sand-filled conical seashell - but no one really knows their origin. Even the most primitive tribes seem to have discovered that a long thorn or a pointed thin twig pushed right through the centre of a large nut or fruit made an excellent finger top.

The method of starting the spin all depends on a top's shape, size and method of manufacture. Small tops that have a thin central spindle or peg can be twirled rapidly between finger and thumb. They are known as **Finger Tops**. **Whip Tops**, however, come in a variety of upside-down cone shapes that can have incised lines around to aid the tight turning of a whipcord. The top, when fully wound on to the whip can be launched in several different

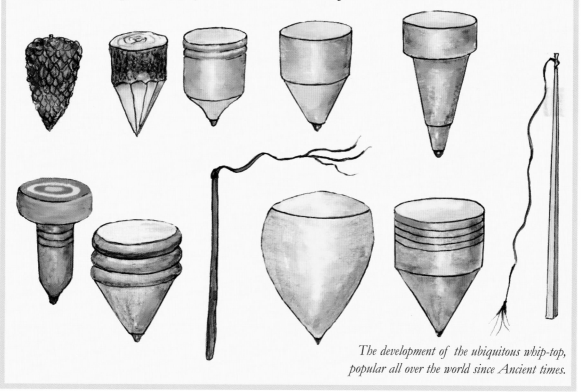

The development of the ubiquitous whip-top, popular all over the world since Ancient times.

Drawings showing children from different periods of history enjoying whip and top.

ways. First, both whip and top are held in one hand, then, as the hand is rapidly flicked forwards and back the top is released. The sudden unwinding of the cord creates the spin, which can be kept up by continued whipping. Another way to launch is by holding the wound-up top upright in one hand, between the upturned first and second fingers with the tip of the thumb on the centre. The whip is held in the other hand, then as it is pulled back sharply spin is applied to the top. Many elderly people have related to me how they used this hold, but the point of the top would be placed into a crack in a paving slab or cobblestone to help hold it still. They also described how a whip top was made uniquely theirs by the added decoration of chalked colours, foil sweet-wrappers or a shiny drawing-pin stuck into the top. Whip tops had many names, such as Granny, Turnip, Carrot, Beehive, Torpedo and many more. Many places used to have a Parish Top, an extremely large whip top that required a strong whipping arm to keep it going. People used it during frosty weather as a way of keeping their circulation going. (Bring them back, I say.)

In the mid-eighteenth century woodworking machinery improved to include the lathes on which the more refined **Peg Tops** were turned from both local and foreign hardwoods. Very early woodcuts and paintings from around the world show this type of top in use. The launching cord needs to be both thin and strong with a large knot or bead at the pulling end for grip. To launch,

hold the top upside down with the cord wound tightly round from the point to the widest part ensuring that no crossovers occur. Then throw the top forcefully forwards from head high ending with a sudden jerk backwards. To my dismay I have never mastered the technique, but it seems to come naturally to most children.

In Asia and other Eastern countries peg tops became **Fighting Tops**, deliberately aimed to split and destroy the tops of opponents. In Japan and China, many street entertainers performed wonderful tricks with them, and many illustrations depict children catching rapidly revolving peg tops on the palm of their hand. Some Japanese and Chinese tops are very large, almost like dinner plates; rolling the peg between the palms of the hands launches these. In Malaysia, extremely large spinning tops that have heavy metal tyres around the circumference are used competitively by teams of men from neighbouring communities. They are launched by a sharp pull from a very long cord on to flat-topped clay mounds, where they spin for ages. The top that spins for the longest time is the winner.

Launcher Tops come in a variety of shapes, but all have a tall central peg with a hole drilled through to take thin cord. Most have a wooden handle or launcher with a hole or a slot in the end to accommodate the peg loosely. The peg is placed in the handle, one end of the cord is pushed a little way through the hole in the peg and the top is spun to wind it in. To launch, the

Left: A Japanese boy using a traditional launcher top or 'Comma'.
Below: Alternative ways of making finger tops, they can be used for colour mixing experiments and to demonstrate centrifugal force. Easy to make from card circles and short pencils.

handle is held tightly in one hand and the remaining end of the cord in the other with the top about 5cm above a table or other flat surface. A long, strong pull will cause the top to spin at an amazing rate for a long time. Right up until today many different games have been invented and sold incorporating this kind of spinner, the latest being the Bey Blade, a fancy (all-bells-and-whistles) plastic version of a 1950s Japanese spinning top game called Bei-Goma. These have been heavily promoted in the media and sold worldwide for a few years now. I have found, however, that children can have just as much fun with the simple wooden launcher tops featured here. On some, the launcher is incorporated into the side of the box or frame. Most of these games incorporate miniature skittles or have holes into which a top can fall, thereby scoring points.

Any spinning top that has a flat top can be used to demonstrate the scientific theory of light and colour mixing. Just cut a set of card circles, then mark across the centre line with a pencil. First, fill halves with primary colours - red-yellow, red-blue, and so on. When these are spun, onlookers will be amazed at the result. Have fun experimenting with other colour combinations: try bright colours around the circumference of the circles. Finally, carefully mark one card circle into seven equal segments and fill each segment with the exact colours of the rainbow, namely red, orange, yellow, green, blue, indigo and violet. The blue needs to be a mid-blue and indigo a rich dark blue; keep the colouring as neat as possible for best results. Now, ask yourself what colour a rainbow is when it is spun. The result may amaze you. Did you guess correctly? When you know the answer, allow others to find out on their own.

One of the best spinning top games I know is one that I christened **the Dubliner** after a lady of that city who told me all about it. She described how, in the 1930s, she and her friends would set a (cord-launched) top spinning on a tray or a plate. They then had great fun passing it from tray to tray, or plate to plate. I decided to adapt the idea and use another similar idea from the early nineteenth century. I enlisted the help of a very good friend known as Taro the Jester - the stage name of Stuart Fell, a well-known stunt man who also performs amazing tricks with a whole variety of spinning tops, scarily close to his audiences. Between us we devised the toy illustrated, essentially a handheld bat the handle of which forms a cord launcher. A turned wooden cup is glued on to one edge of the bat. A variety of skills are required to master this game. First, launch the top on to a flat smooth surface or floor, then after the spinning has smoothed out scoop the top up and on to the bat in one continuous movement. If you hold the bat steady and perfectly flat the top will continue to spin in its centre. The next trick is to practise flicking the still-spinning top from one side of the bat to the other. When this stage has been mastered, flip the top into the air in an attempt to catch it (still spinning) into the shallow cup. It is great fun and I challenge anyone to master this old-time game. To make it, just follow what you see in the illustrations. The handle need not be lathe-turned: a smooth stick drilled and then cut as a top launcher will do. To make working spinning tops, owning a wood-turning lathe is not essential. Over the centuries tops have been fashioned from short lengths of perfectly round tree branch, a sharp knife or axe being the only tool required. During the Depression home toy makers would carefully use a penknife to make a conical point on one end of a wooden cotton reel; an old pencil or a dowel passed through the centre hole formed the point.

Making small finger tops is relatively easy: pass a sharpened stick, cocktail stick, dowel, and so on, through the centre of a card or wood

My 'Dublinner' launcher top/catch game, developed from an early Irish game of passing a top between tea trays (see text for details.

circle, a seed or nut and you will have an excellent toy. **Tee-To-Tums** are finger tops that are made hexagonal, each flat side being numbered just like a dice. The tee-to-tum was used in children's games in preference to the gambling influence of regular dice. The traditional Jewish Dreidel top has meaningful sayings around its edge; it is used during the annual Jewish festival of Hanukkah. Some finger tops are shaped like little people wearing tall, thin hats; they have tiny arms loosely hung from the shoulders. When the top is spun, the arms fly outwards and upwards under the influence of centrifugal force. Others are made hollow so that on being spun they whistle or hum, or they might have a set of shiny, bent-wire profiles which when spun appear as solid faces or objects.

During the nineteenth century many board games incorporated cord-launched spinning tops as part of the action. Some knocked down miniature skittles, others struck sets of coloured marbles. I have a very quirky version that knocks coloured ping-pong balls randomly off wire stands. Make a simple launcher top, then go on to invent a similar game. A plastic tea tray makes an excellent playing area; baffles and scoring areas can be stuck down with Araldite epoxy resin adhesive. Being able to turn wood, even on a primitive pole lathe, will enable a maker to produce excellent spinning tops of all kinds.

Many toys are directly related to tops because they are launched in a similar way, and they rely on their spinning to amuse and amaze, therefore I include them in this section. One of the earliest recorded is the **Egg Mill** or **Nut Mill**, which is featured in many paintings and illustrations between 1550 and 1700. These show a turned wooden egg shape being held in one hand while the other holds the end of a cord

The 17th Century vertical cord pull mill (see egg mill p 111).

that is wrapped around the spindle of a horizontal wooden cross. The Brueghel painting clearly shows a version with three revolving crosses. The repeated pulling and slackening of the cord initiates and then continues a back-and-forth rotation of the cross or crosses due to the flywheel effect and centrifugal force. A similar but more spectacular toy followed this invention: someone, somewhere, added a twisted, propeller-like blade to the top of the spindle. The rotational forces, combined with the lifting, screw effect of the propeller blades, force the revolving mass to fly upwards in a helicopter-like vertical take-off. The Japanese version of this toy is the Taketombo, which is described in the Flying Toys section. Revolving propellers can be dangerous if not used sensibly. Remember that a propeller that is revolved the wrong way will be forced to fly downwards or backwards. Be aware of your own and other people's safety. Adult supervision is recommended.

The Tudor egg mill, the flywheel action keeps the heavy wooden vanes spinning back and forth if used properly (See the 'Children's Games' painting p. 66-67).

The Whizzer or **Puddle Cutter** (also known as **Buzz Saw** or **Colour Mixer**) could also fit equally well in the Whistles and Noisemakers section. The Ancient Greeks certainly knew well this simple spinning disc suspended from a doubled cord, and it is still popular today. It was a favourite toy during Victorian times and also during the Second World War, when we used to make them from coat buttons. The toy consists of a disc with two holes just spanning the centre; it can be made from thin ply, MDF, plastic sheet, a tin lid, thick card or a very large, flat, coat button. Whichever materials you choose, all the discs will need two small holes straddling the centre point 3cm-4cm apart, and a cord passing through to form a continuous loop. The addition of bamboo or bead handles prevents the strong cord from cutting into the fingers. One of my nineteenth-century books tells and shows how puddle cutters could be made from a large circle of lead cut to look just like a circular saw blade. Apparently, the game was to dip the rapidly spinning disc into a puddle thereby splashing yourself and your

pals: the puddle cutter in action. As a child I remember making the buzz saw version from a tin lid; it made a wonderful noise as it cut through a sheet of tightly stretched newspaper. Try making holes around the circumference: you will find that different sizes produce different kinds of whistling or humming noises. The smaller button type suspended on cotton thread was ideal for tangling up in the hair of an unsuspecting victim (not recommended).

To make a whizzer work, hold the ends of the loop over two hands, palms inwards. Give the disc a start by moving your hands in a forward circular motion: this will cause the disc to revolve and the cord to twist up. Once this happens, gently pull your hands apart, forcing the disc to spin even faster, then as soon as you feel a little resistance allow the cord to wind the other way under the centrifugal flywheel effect. Repeating this action will cause the disc to spin even faster in both directions. A few holes drilled through the disc should cause a loud whizzing or humming noise. The colour experiments described in the Spinning Tops and Toys section can all be done on a set of whizzers. As with cricket, hockey and golf balls, spinning discs and flat sections of board can be dangerous if not played with within safety rules. Common sense should dictate where and how any spinning toy is used.

Three versions of the well known and easy to make spinner, the top one is made from tin and will cut paper, the others can be heavy card or wood. 1940s children used to make them with large coat buttons.

Tip-Cat, Bat and Trap, Battledore and Shuttlecock

All the games in this section are best played outdoors, and all require a bat of some kind. **The Tip-Cat** is the oldest of the set: it was used centuries ago as an aid to developing good hand-eye coordination. It is simple to make and consists of a 12cm-long section of 4cm-diameter tree branch that is sharpened to a blunt point at both ends. A longer length of suitable branch is used as a bat. Like many ancient games, the rules can differ from place to place. To play, the striker or batsman places the tip-cat on to a flat surface, then stands to one side and attempts to strike one of the pointed ends with the end of his bat. If he is successful the tip-cat will rise upwards, turning over and over; and as it does so it must be struck forwards as hard as possible. The furthest hit or series of hits can be added together to find the winner. Alternatively, a target peg or a horizontal target can be aimed for.

A selection of 'Tip-Cats', 'Bat and Catty' or 'Pig and Stick' a very old favourite revived for children during WWII.

A very similar game known as **Nipsy** was played until recently by miners in fields around the Yorkshire town of Barnsley as a Sunday morning team game. The nipsy consists of a hardwood (Lignum-Vitae) egg shape that has a flat segment sliced from the underside at one end. The flattened section makes it act just like a tip-cat when struck by a long whippy nipsy stick fashioned from a steam-treated pick handle (it looks rather like a double-headed golf club). For ease of recognition each team has a different coloured spot dabbed on their nipsies. To play, the captains toss a coin to decide which team gets first strike. The player places his nipsy on to one end of a house brick that has been heeled into the ground. Then, holding tightly to

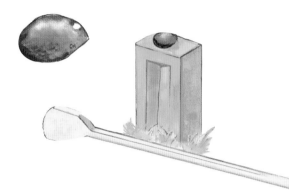

The Yorkshire miner's game of 'Nipsy' a derivative of tip-cat (see text).

A trapball or bat and trap, another derivative of tip-cat, very popular from medieval times.

the handle of his stick he attempts to strike the rear end of the nipsy, thereby forcing it to rise gracefully into the air. If successful, he whacks the spinning nipsy forwards forcefully. The team members take turns to strike the furthest; the distances are measured by reeling out a thin rope that has a knot tied at every yard or metre. The individual hits are added together and the team that has hit the furthest overall buys the drinks in the pub until lunchtime. One of the last teams to play nipsy in Barnsley presented me with a specially made nipsy and a steam-pressed nipsy stick just a few years ago.

The Bat and Trap (also know as Trap Ball) is a very similar game, the only difference being that a small wooden ball is placed on the end of a finely balanced trigger, and striking the trigger with a wooden bat makes the ball rise just like a tip-cat. A medieval woodcut clearly shows one fashioned from the forked branch of a tree (see illustration). In the sixteenth century traps were fashioned in the shape of shoes that had a protruding wooden tongue as the trigger, a design that continued to the end of the nineteenth century. When a small wooden or leather-bound ball is placed into the leg of the shoe the weight depresses the wooden trigger. Many illustrations show this exciting game being enjoyed; one depicts a bat and trap among gifts presented to a Chinese Emperor or high-ranking official. The related game of Knurr and Spell was developed in the eighteenth century; the only difference was that the whole thing was constructed mainly from iron, and it had a quick-release steel spring to launch the ball.

Battledore and Shuttlecock, the forerunner of tennis-type games, seems to have been passed down from China and Japan. Many medieval woodcuts show players happily striking a feathered missile back and forth with small wooden bats. In the Middle Ages the Horn Book was devised as an educational tool, consisting of a handheld bat shape that had letters, numbers and prayers carved into or stuck on to the flat surfaces. Transparent sheet horn was used to protect the printed papers, hence the name. Schoolchildren of the time soon learned that their horn book could be used as a bat for a game of battledore and shuttlecock. Later, during the more educationally enlightened times of the eighteenth century, a link was made with these horn book-battledores and basic reading books for small children became referred to as battledores. They consisted of a few card pages printed with alphabets, word lists and a short story or fable along with a simple illustration or two; sadly they couldn't be used to bash a shuttlecock back and forth.

Medieval and 18th Century versions of trapball.

 A number of other games can be played with a single shuttlecock: a single player might practise repeatedly hitting it upwards while keeping a score of hits. Another good game is to set a small hoop on the ground (or mark out a circle) and the players launch their shuttlecocks high into the air with the aim of getting closest to the centre. More skill is required to play Cock-a-Hoop, where the shuttlecock is thrown back and forth through a hoop being rolled between an opposing team. As with many old games, you can make up the rules to suit yourself. More proof that cheap-to-make old-time toys and games can give lots of fun to all age groups.

A Medieval/Tudor horn book and battledore and shuttlecock, a combination of learning and fun.

Drawings showing how battledore and shuttlecock was enjoyed by different cultures and across history

To make the bat is an easy task: traditionally it would have been fashioned from a thin board of any local hardwood, whereas today any suitable ply or MDF can be used; it all depends on how traditional you wish to be. Shop-bought shuttlecocks are very cheap and easy to obtain, but it will be far more satisfying to make your own. All you require are a few sections of 25mm-diameter tree branch (or broom-stale) about 25mm long. Use a 3mm drill to make four holes in the top of each to take the feathers. You can usually find suitable feathers during walks in the countryside or in city parks; if not, you can get them from crafts suppliers. Stick the four feathers (with the natural curl outwards and downwards) using an adhesive to hold them in place, then trim them neatly across the top with sharp scissors. When they are dry you can enjoy the clickety-clacking game of old-time battledore and shuttlecock.

Toys That Amaze and Puzzle

Among these are the Hookey, the Spider-in-a-Packet and Flipping Frog tricks described elsewhere in the book. However, here are three more simple-to-make toys with which to amaze all and sundry. One of the easiest is the **Magic Propeller** or **Gee-Haw** (it gets called many other names): all that you need are three lengths of dowel or tree branch. First, cut about 20cm of 10mm-15mm dowel or stick, then use a sharp penknife, file or even the edge of a grindstone to form a series of even V-shaped grooves two thirds along its length. Next, cut 60cm of 4mm or 5mm dowel and drill a hole through dead centre to take a thin nail. Use a knife or sanding belt to taper gradually inwards towards the centre so that it looks a little like a dumb-bell: this is the propeller. Cutting another 9cm from the 5mm dowel makes a rubbing stick; now

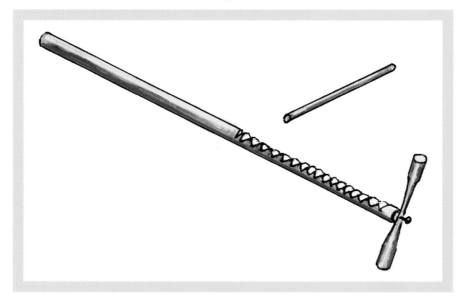

The magic propeller or 'Gee-Haw', a tricky novelty toy that amazes everyone.

*How to operate your
'Gee-Haw'
(Top Secret) see text.*

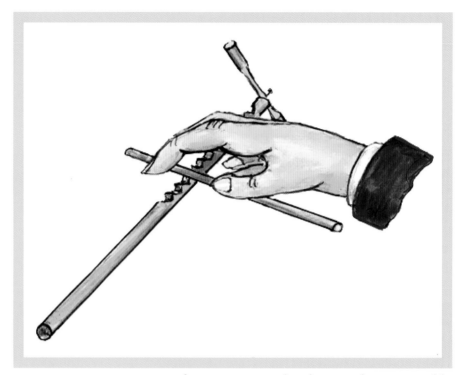

sandpaper any rough edges ready to assemble the toy. First acquire a thin, steel (not brass) panel-pin or nail - preferably one having a flat head - and use a fine bit to pre-drill the dead centre of the grooved dowel (see illustration). Place the propeller on to the nail and carefully hammer it into place, ensuring that it can spin very freely. To make sure that the toy works properly, balance the propeller if it is heavy on one side by sanding a little off the heavy end until perfect equilibrium is achieved.

Now for the fun bit. This requires plenty of rehearsing to get it just right - the operator needs to be a bit of a showman. Hold the grooved stick by the smooth end in one hand, and the rubbing stick exactly in the way shown in my illustration in the other. You will notice that the finger and thumb tips forms a bridge over the grooves. To start, rub the rubbing stick up and down the grooves without either finger or thumb tips touching the sides. Result? The propeller remains stationary. Now try the same thing, but allow just the fingertip to rub the side of the grooved stick. Result? The propeller should revolve merrily one way. Now do the same again, but with only the thumb tip rubbing, to go into reverse.

What you now have, folks, is the only voice-operated wooden toy in the world. On your command that darned propeller will do exactly as it is told - but it will only respond to the voice of the owner. The side-to-side fingertip gear-change movement must be minuscule, and when it is accompanied by a string of meaningless fibs, the onlookers are completely taken in (unless they already know the secret, of course). Like the hookey novelty, you always sell the secret, never give it away. This is an ideal school or craft event project. You could even show off by demonstrating that if two magic propellers are held together crossed over in the middle, when one is rubbed both propellers turn - but in opposite directions. Apparently it all functions through vibration and resonance being biased by dampening. I have seen grown men (even engineers) almost crying with frustration trying to get the darned thing to work. (By the way, why Gee-Haw? Those are the two words drivers of horse-drawn vehicles in nineteenth-century America used to make their horses turn left or right.)

The Sky-Hook is another simple-to-make novelty with which to mystify your friends and family. Please study the picture: you will see that

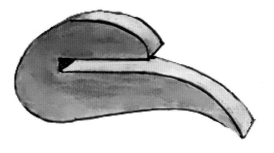

The amazing sky-hook, trouser belt balancing trick, to amaze and amuse your friends.

The Snake in a Box packs a big surprise for the unsuspecting (or nosey) opener. A narrow rectangular box with a lid sliding in a groove contains a specially shaped wooden snake with a flickering rubber tongue. As the lid slides open the head of the snake suddenly pops out and forwards to bite or lick the hand. I have two very old ones in my collection: one Victorian, the other made around the time of the First World War. Neither of these would pass Trading Standards inspection today, since each snake has an extremely sharp needle inserted as a tongue. The later of the two contains a pair of these deadly snakes - and they really bite. This amusing toy can also be found made completely from soft soapstone, usually imported from Africa.

The sneaky snake in a box trick, open the box if you dare!

it consists of a specially shaped hook cut from any suitable board, the whole sized to fit into an adult hand, approximately 9cm by 5cm. Use a fret or scroll saw to cut the shape (the slot needs to be about 5mm wide) then sandpaper all the rough edges until smooth. The trick is to balance the sky-hook by its point on a single fingertip: an impossible task until you incorporate a standard trouser belt, preferably one of leather. Pass the belt through the slot so that the buckle end balances the other. Now when you place the sky-hook on a fingertip the whole will balance, much to the amazement of all doubters.

The Snake in a Box illustrated is the gentler (but just as scary) version of the toy: the evil green snake has an elastic-band tongue. The box is made from 6mm birch ply or MDF; make it comfortable to hold in an adult hand. The wooden snake must be shaped as shown and be narrow enough to revolve loosely about its pivot.

Thread a thin, strong cord through a hole on the

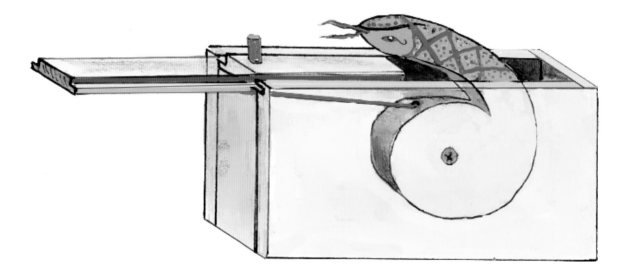

underside of the snake's head, then round and down to be glued and wedged into a hole at about 7 o'clock on the circular body. Glue and staple the other end of the cord in a shallow groove on the underside of the sliding lid. The lid has a short section of 4mm dowel as a pull handle; glue this in at the halfway point to ensure that the holder is well and truly bitten every time.

I have found that it is best to leave the box plain with just a coat of varnish, oil or wax to prevent marking. Cut out the curled-up snake with a fret or scroll saw and shape it on the sanding belt. A groove can be cut for a mouth and a hole drilled to take half a doubled elastic band (bright green or red if possible) that is then glued and wedged to produce the typical forked tongue. Paint the snake with a bright green base coat, then decorate it with crosses, lines and dots to make it look as poisonous as possible; this decoration will only need to cover the parts that are seen as the box is opened. I strongly suggest that you make an undecorated working prototype before proceeding to make a quantity. After all these years, that little snake in a box can pack a real punch: many people go weak at the knees and scream, others recoil in horror. Most children laugh it off but a few show an innate aversion to the box's contents. No harm done - in fact, because it is amusing it can actually help cure an aversion.

A typical Victorian 'Jack-in-the-Box', easy to make if you can find a suitable metal spring. One from an old chair?

Street Toys

A number of wooden toys are difficult to categorize, and though their origins are not recorded most are known worldwide. **Clompers** (the Dutch word for clogs), for example, are simply a pair of wooden blocks that have holes for a long string loop. The blocks can be made from any suitable wood, even logs flattened on two sides. (A similar toy was very popular in the first half of the twentieth century but made from two large tins.) Children love to clomp around wearing adult shoes, and this is just a variation of that.

To make a pair, just cut and shape the blocks to suit the age and ability of the child. Then drill holes for the cord corner-ways through the block that is below the instep (see illustration).

Clompers are almost certainly derived from the ancient game of stilt walking. **Stilts** have been used both in work and play throughout their history: farmers have used them in hop fields for centuries, and circus and street performers still use them today. (The Brueghel painting depicts a pair in use.) Stilts are easily made from two lengths of suitable timber, which must have no knots or short grain that might cause them to break. All edges and corners need to be sanded smooth; roughly shaped grips can be carved at the top of each one. The foot-rests need to be fixed very securely with glue and screws at a height to suit the user. Like all games of balance, practice makes perfect, and I recommend that beginners start on a clear area of soft turf.

Above: A pair of home-made Clompers, a great favourite of children during WWII, they can also be made from two empty golden syrup or (small) paint tins. Right: A typical pair of stilts, they can be made in all sizes but must be splinter free.

The Flipper Dinger is a strange and amusing item, consisting of a hollow tube fashioned from hedgerow elder or even hollowed-out bamboo; as long as the tube is hollow and plugged at one end it will work fine. One look at my picture should explain all. Drill the tube a little way in from the plugged end to take a thinner tube: it will look a little like a chimney. Use a length of stiff wire for a miniature basketball hoop, fixed behind the small upright tube. Now for the tricky bit, for which you need a very lightweight ball - you can get one from a craft shop or make one from elder pith, or even soft tissue paper dampened then rolled tightly into a ball. Use thin nose pliers to bend a hook on one end of a short length of thin wire; push the straight end through the ball, then bend it back up and in to fix it permanently. The flipper dinger is great fun: blow through the tube just enough to get that hooked ball airborne, then try to get it hooked over that wire loop - easy ain't it? Who needs a Game Boy!

The Jacobs Ladder is a novelty toy based on a Bible story and has an extremely long history. It can be found made from many different materials throughout the world, and is relatively easy to make from any scrap board and a couple of lengths of colourful ribbon or cloth tape. First, you will need to cut and sandpaper a set of

The fabulous 'Flipper-Dinger' a favourite Folk Toy from the USA (see text for details).

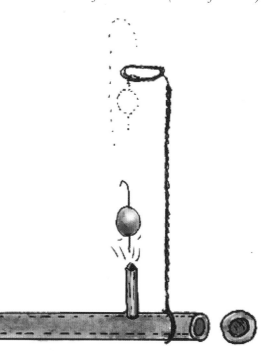

123

5cm-square wooden blocks cut from a board around 6mm thick. Each block must have both ends rounded slightly, then sanded and decorated in any way that you wish. Cut the ribbon into 14cm lengths, and then great care

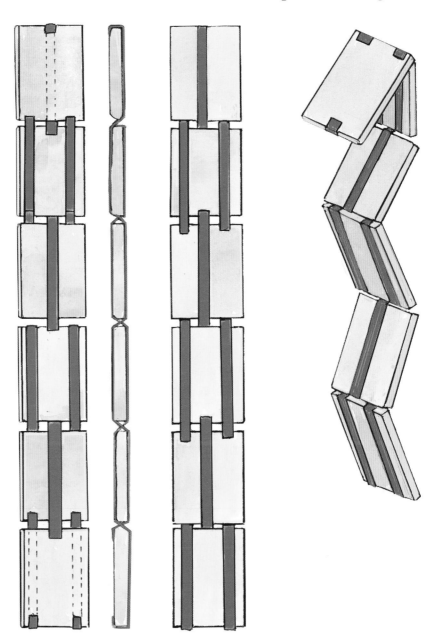

The 'Jacob's Ladder' falling blocks, gravity toy, a real puzzler!

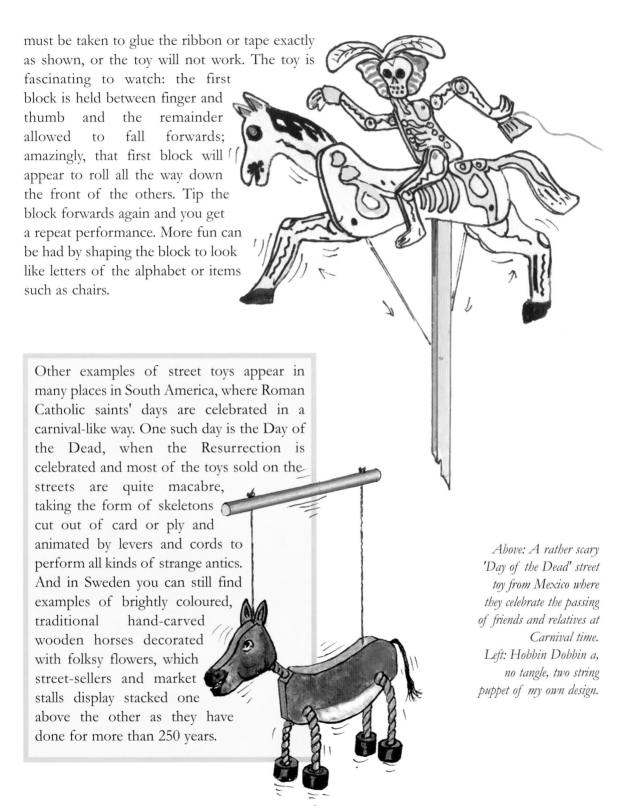

must be taken to glue the ribbon or tape exactly as shown, or the toy will not work. The toy is fascinating to watch: the first block is held between finger and thumb and the remainder allowed to fall forwards; amazingly, that first block will appear to roll all the way down the front of the others. Tip the block forwards again and you get a repeat performance. More fun can be had by shaping the block to look like letters of the alphabet or items such as chairs.

Other examples of street toys appear in many places in South America, where Roman Catholic saints' days are celebrated in a carnival-like way. One such day is the Day of the Dead, when the Resurrection is celebrated and most of the toys sold on the streets are quite macabre, taking the form of skeletons cut out of card or ply and animated by levers and cords to perform all kinds of strange antics. And in Sweden you can still find examples of brightly coloured, traditional hand-carved wooden horses decorated with folksy flowers, which street-sellers and market stalls display stacked one above the other as they have done for more than 250 years.

Above: A rather scary 'Day of the Dead' street toy from Mexico where they celebrate the passing of friends and relatives at Carnival time.
Left: Hobbin Dobbin a, no tangle, two string puppet of my own design.

The Dala Horse was first produced in Sweden in the 1700's.

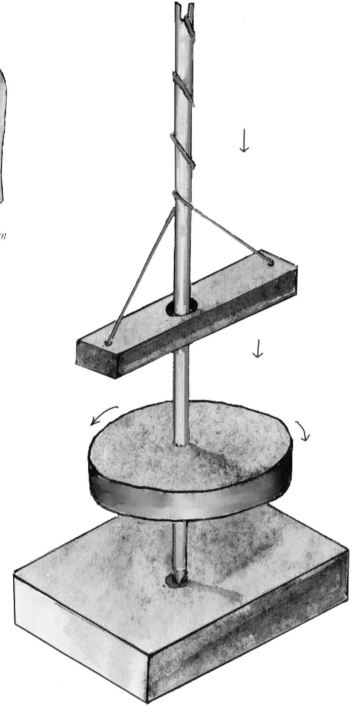

A 'Smoke Grinder' a Folk Toy from the U.S.A. based upon a Native Indian fire maker or drill, it uses a flywheel action via a twisted cord

The Smoke Grinder, once used by native American Indians, is more of a tool than a toy. The simple rotary action combined with a flywheel effect was used to create fire and even drill holes. Today it is sold to tourists as an all-American folk toy. Try making one yourself: you will be amazed at how efficient it is when used properly.

In many countries, the crudest of wooden street toys continue to add happiness to the lives of children deprived by famine or war. **The Log Cow** is a good example. The **Wooden Hippopotamus** was fashioned from a fallen branch, carved a little, and then decorated in the stylised manner shown. The simple two-weight balancer can be made from sections of tree branch as shown, or from lumps of soft clay allowed to harden in the sun.

A beautifully simple pull toy fashioned from half a log, fantastic for on the beach?.

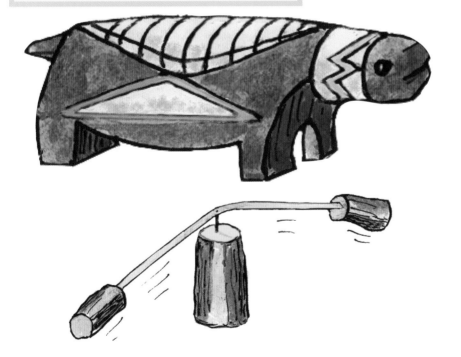

Top left: A true Folk Toy from Africa, with typical ornamentation. Below left: A simple two weight balancer.

127

Whistles, Rattles and Noisemakers

I will start by describing whistles that are simple hollow tubes. The longer the tube the deeper the note produced; the shorter the tube the higher the note. The size and shape of a whistle also affects its pitch: hedgerow branches produce good whistles, the elder especially because the soft pith found within early summer growth can be pushed out easily. Likewise, bamboo of all diameters can be used. Solid sticks, especially those cut from fruit trees with secateurs, are ideal but these need to be drilled. Block one end of almost any tube, blow across the open end, and you should hear a breathy note. Fixing a row of eight to ten hollow tubes together (diminishing in size) produces a passable set of **Pan-Pipes**.

The many ways of making wooden whistles that work (se text for details).

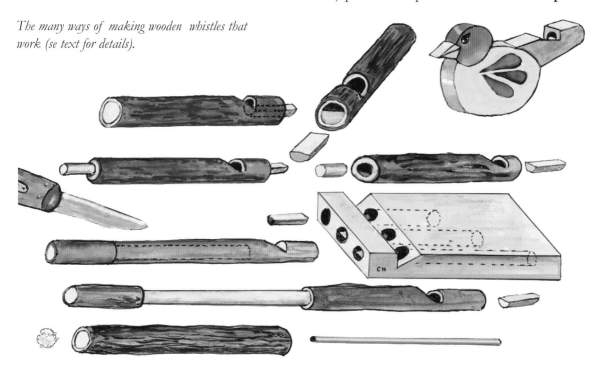

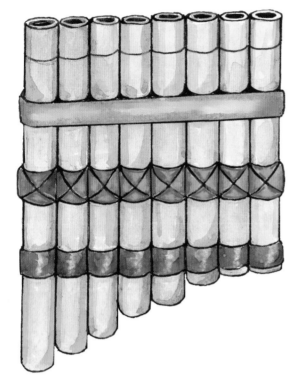

A set of bamboo 'Pan Pipes' from the Andes, just hollow tubes of diminishing length, blown across the top.

Next, whistles with a hole known as the window and sill - that is, a small oblong hole with a slope the thin end of which faces the mouthpiece. In this case, the simple hollow tube is fully blocked at one end; a natural node (bamboo or elder) can be used, or a cork or wooden plug. Alternatively, you can drill a solid dowel or suitable stick to a chosen depth. Great care must be taken and the use of a vice is highly recommended. My illustrations feature a whole variety of wooden whistles. You will note that the mouthpiece end requires that the hole be filled with a short half-round section of dowel or stick. The blown air is forced over this on to the thin edge of the sill, vibrating the air to produce a note. A little experimentation will pay dividends: after a few attempts you will become an efficient maker of working wooden whistles. The basic whistle,

The origins of whistles, rattles and other noise-producing toys are lost in the mists of time. We know that the Ancient Egyptians, Greeks and Romans used many different types made from all kinds of materials, though mostly from wood or baked clay. And noisemakers remain popular to this day: toddlers love to hold a noisy rattle or, as they get older, blow a whistle or beat a toy drum. Most instruments that make music and rhythm come from simple beginnings: the first rattles were hollow seed gourds, and the first whistles from hollow reeds or straw. As craft skills and tools improved, people learned that whistles of different lengths and drums and rattles differing in size produced notes, and this led to the birth of music. Rattles, whistles and other noisemakers were used not only for celebrations but also to help ward off evil spirits. Two Brueghel paintings depict Lenten Rattles (see page 132), which were used at Easter instead of bells.

once mastered, can be altered to give different notes and pitch; a number of correctly placed finger holes can produce a passable recorder-like instrument. Multiple holes drilled into a block will sound a chord; tuned properly they can sound just like an old-time American steam locomotive.

Produce a whistle with a tightly fitting slider and you get a **Swannee whistle** whose note rises and falls in a most amusing manner as the slide is pushed and pulled. This type of whistle has been a favourite for centuries, and they are easily made from the spring growth of the ash tree. Cut a long length of suitable branch between the black buds; use a sharp penknife to cut just through the bark all round about 3cm from one end - this forms the slider handle. Now for the tricky bit: use the handle of your penknife to tap-tap gently all the way up and down and around the longest

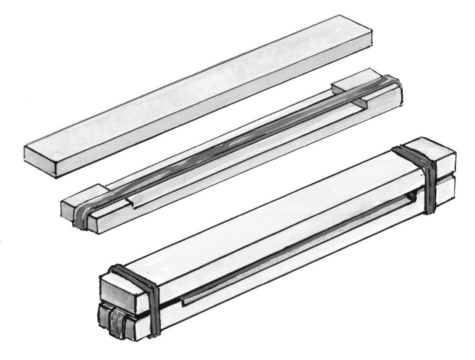

A large version of 'Mr Punch's' Swazzle or squeaky voice, a very wide elastic band forms the reed that makes it work.

section of bark. The tapping bruises the soft pliable bark (you need to be very patient or it will split) and eventually you will find that with a gentle pull the encircling bark will slide off the stick. Cut about 4cm off the shiny white stick that is left. Use the offcut to make the half-round plug, and use the hollow bark tube as your whistle. Very carefully, cut a window in the bark then insert the tightly fitting plug; then block the other end with a finger and give it a test blow. When a clear note sounds, push the slider portion back into place: now you can have lots of fun making all kinds of weird noises.

The distinctive voice of Mr Punch is made through a tiny instrument known as a **Swazzle**, a homemade device held in the mouth of the puppeteer. The expertise to make a genuine swazzle is a secret well kept by genuine Punch and Judy performers. I will now describe a simple-to-make noisemaker very similar in sound to the swazzle but larger in construction. Cut two 10cm lengths of 10mm-15mm square section timber; on the top face of one use a fine saw to cut squarely across about 15mm in from each end and only 2mm deep (see diagram). Use a scroll saw or a sharp knife to cut out the long section between the cuts ensuring that it is flat and not more than 2mm deep. Because this item is blown it needs to be sanded until very smooth all round. Find a wide elastic band and stretch it from end to end of the block that has been cut. Place this face down on to the plain block and join them together using two small elastic bands wrapped around each end. Your noisemaker is now complete: the wide elastic band has become a vibrating reed or tongue and when you place your lips around the blocks (like a mouth organ)

In America and Canada many woodsmen make their own hunting calls, and these can sound realistically like the hunted duck, goose or moose. The size and shape of the whistle with the addition of reeds helps produce the most amazing sounds. The bird whistle illustrated is just one of the many alternative shapes that can be cut from wood. Many old-time toys made in Germany and Eastern Europe featured animals and birds with a working whistle as a tail. There are many specialist books on making whistles and wooden wind instruments (including organ pipes). If you are keen to make more, I suggest you read and study them.

A beautifully designed 'Cuckoo' whistle from 19th Century Germany, the bird tips forward to cover a second hole to sound the other note.

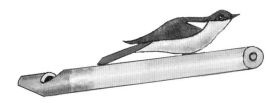

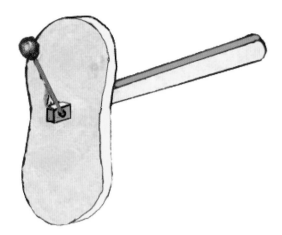

A medieval 'Lenten Rattle' as used in Lenten processions instead of bells.

and blow, you should produce a loud rasping noise, very much like that produced by a blade of grass held between the thumbs. The note and pitch is dependent on the depth of slot and type of elastic band used. With a little practice, you will soon learn how to speak through the instrument and talk with a very raucous Mr Punch voice.

Clapper rattles are easily made from any suitable flat board. First, mark out then cut a basic square or rectangular bat shape complete with integral handle. Next, use the bat as a template to mark out then cut a pair of matching plates; the rattle will be louder if large shallow holes are carved or drilled into the meeting faces. Cramp all three pieces together and drill two holes right through just above the handle. Thread a leather thong or strong cord through the holes in order that all three sections are held together so that they clap when shaken.

A Japanese clapper rattle, plain ones made much larger were used as bird scarers in Europe for centuries. They can also be used for stage sound effects.

Throughout history people have used rattles of all kinds. At first, found items such as hollow seed gourds or seashells threaded on to a cord were used. Since then, growing ingenuity and improving tools and skills have produced many different kinds. In Ancient Egypt, a sacred rattle or Sistrum was used - one found in the tomb of Tutankhamun has a metal frame with wires and metal discs fitted into a gilded wooden handle. When shaken it produces a distinctive metallic sound that is ideal for use during religious ceremonies. Ancient China and Japan produced the earliest Clapper Rattles, which consist of one or more flat wooden plates tied loosely to a bat-like handle. When shaken sharply up and down they produce a very loud clapping sound, which gets louder if shallow hollows are drilled or carved into the plates. Almost every tribe, civilization and community has embraced the use of rattles and noisemakers. They were once used to warn of the approach of a leper in place of a hand-bell; they have been used as processional noisemakers in place of bells at Easter in Roman Catholic countries and as percussion instruments in bands and orchestras in general; in Britain they also made very effective bird-scarers right up until the late nineteenth century, usually wielded by small boys who would be paid a pittance to trudge around frosty, muddy fields for hours on end. During both World Wars loud rattles (mainly the rotary type) were used by wardens to warn of imminent air-raid or poisonous gas attack. Even today rattles are used in some American skyscrapers as warning instruments in case of fire alarm failure. And in street theatre, puppeteers and showmen all use noisemakers to produce sound effects, such as the whistling of the wind, the sounds of horses' hooves or the ghostly rattle of chains.

A novelty noisemaker with whistles made by paper bellows from 19th Century Germany.

The Rotary Rattle consists of a thin, wide tongue of hardwood the end of which is in contact with a rotating star or cogwheel, which produces a very loud rasping noise as the whole rattle is pivoted on the handle. Rotary rattles have a long and interesting history, and feature in many engravings and pictures. One woodcut shows Tudor children enjoying using one. They were used during both World Wars as a warning of a gas attack or air raid, and right up until the late 1970s, many British soccer fans rattled them when their team scored a goal. (The less pleasant plastic air-horn replaced them.) The ones in my collection were once used with Swannee whistles during performances of Leopold Mozart's 'Toy Symphony' in Pittsburgh, Pennsylvania, USA, in 1918. A rotary rattle is sometimes used in the ballet Coppélia to make the noise of a key turning the clockwork of the mechanical doll. These are a little more complicated to make and there are many different designs of frame, handle and star wheel.

The illustration shows how to make a **rotary rattle** contained in my collection. Cut two identical strips of wood: these form the top and bottom of the frame. Drill a 9mm hole with the centre 15mm in from one end. (If you are making a quantity, a large block machined to size could be drilled and then ripped into a number of these parts.) Next, cut a solid block of hardwood (this is the end block) then saw a 2mm-wide cut 2cm deep across the centre of one end. Cut the wide tongue to the same width as the end block, then rip it right down the centre to within 3cm of the end. Next, turn a stubby wooden handle (it could be whittled) so that it swivels in the holes in the frame strips. Now the tricky part: cut a short square block to fit neatly between the top and bottom strips, and use this to carve or fashion the cog-like toothed wheel that helps to make the noise (see illustration). Alternatively, you could turn a suitable spindle on the lathe and then cut it into short lengths ready for the cog teeth to be carefully chiselled out. A much easier way for the less skilled operator is simply to glue two suitable blocks together corner-ways to form an eight-point star profile, as illustrated. When the cog or star shape is finished drill a 9mm hole through the centre for it to fit tightly over the handle or spindle between the top and bottom strips.

After sanding, assemble the rattle as follows: push the handle through the bottom strip, then glue on the cogwheel (be sparing with the glue: excess will prevent the toy turning) then fit the top strip. Glue the tongue strip into the end block as shown, then using pins and glue assemble the whole as shown. You will almost certainly have to adjust the length of the split

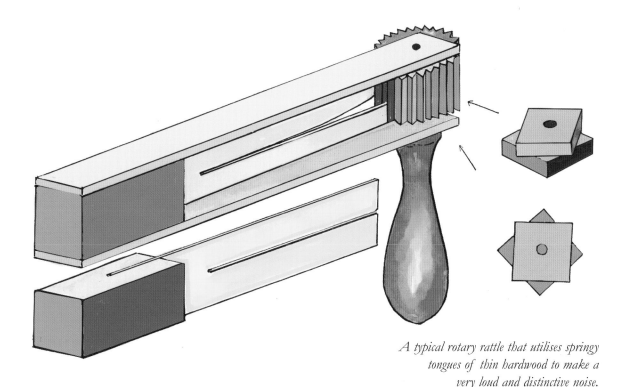

A typical rotary rattle that utilises springy tongues of thin hardwood to make a very loud and distinctive noise.

tongue so that it remains at the deepest point of the cog at dead centre; slight bevels will help the rattle to work smoothly. Allow the glue to dry overnight then try the rattle by holding it in one hand and swinging it around the handle spindle. It should turn in either direction while producing its very distinctive sound. The same basic mechanism was used to produce the sound of a machine gun in many toys during the Second World War: a cranked handle turned the cog against a thin tongue of wood.

The Bull Roarer is almost as old as the human race. The Australian Aborigine and many other primitive tribes used them to scare away enemies and evil spirits. These toys kick up a heck of a racket, and are easy to make. They consist of nothing more than a 4mm-thick wooden board cut to about 15cm by 6cm. Drill a hole to take a

To make the **bull roarer** work, you need a large open space all round, well away from anyone or anything. Wrap the loose end of the cord around your hand and whirl the roarer round and round your head as fast as possible. The air resistance, together with the twirling cord, forces the thin board to spin very quickly, setting up a long, blood-curdling low roaring noise as it does. For safety reasons always demonstrate it in a clear area well away from spectators; the cord needs to be very strong and the knots tied tightly. A modern version might work well turning on a small swivel joint like the ones used for rod fishing.

An Aborigine bull roarer from Australia, a noisemaker toy revived by children during WWII (see text),

Popguns are great fun, easily made and completely harmless if used as instructed; they also memorably demonstrate how the force of compression works, and are an ideal project for a fun science lesson. Popguns were one of the favourite toys of Victorian boys of all social classes. Richer boys used beautifully turned beechwood ones, decorated with bands of bright colours, and manufactured in Germany. A long string tied to the cork prevented it from flying too far. Poorer boys had just as much fun with the homemade hedgerow variety that was made from a large-diameter stick of elder.

long length of strong cord centrally at one end; tie the cord very tight to the roarer. The board can be left plain, have burned designs or be brightly painted.

I will describe how to make the hedgerow version of the **popgun** first. Cut a straight length of elder branch around 15mm-20mm in diameter, then use a series of thinner twigs to push out the centre core of soft pith: save this. Find and cut another (solid) species of straight branch that slides tightly into the now hollow elder one. The two together form the barrel and piston of a very efficient popgun. Victorian boys would happily chew the saved pith or even wads of newspaper to make suitable ammunition, but we must use dampened paper towel or kitchen roll for hygiene's sake. Two wads of wet tissue are pushed tightly into the hollow barrel, then the solid piston is pushed forcibly causing one wad to be ejected with great force and a loud, satisfying POP! In the past, boys could be seen wearing a flat board around their necks like huge lockets. These were chest protectors: the crude popgun was easier to use if the piston was pushed rapidly backwards on to the board. (I won't mention peashooters.)

A more modern variety of popgun (both pistol and rifle) can be made from suitable lengths of easily acquired grey, plastic water pipe, and stock wooden dowel of a size that fits as tightly as possible inside the bore; most DIY stores sell both items. You will also need an old leather belt or a small sheet of thick rubber. First, cut the pipe to the selected length then smooth the sawn ends with sandpaper. Next, cut the wooden dowel to be at least 15cm longer, then smooth

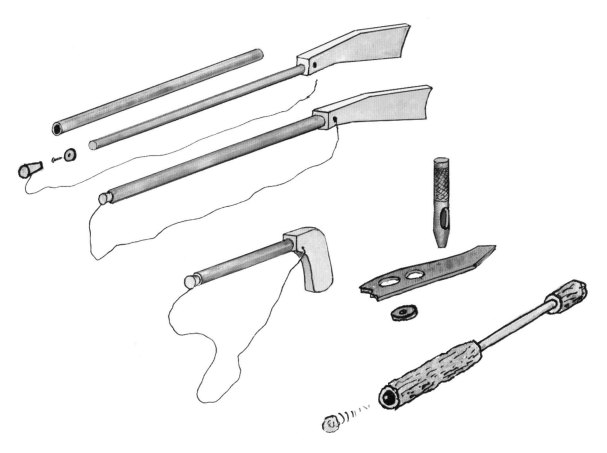

the ends. On to one end of the dowel fit a shaped pistol butt or rifle stock (made easily from any suitable scrap board). With a leather punch or a sharp penknife (children need help with this) make a leather or rubber washer to screw on to the other end of the dowel. The washer must be a very tight sliding fit inside the plastic pipe. You should now have what looks and sounds like a bicycle pump. Find a cork from a wine bottle; it may need sanding all round so that it fits tightly into the end of the plastic barrel. Drill through the thicker end of the cork, tie and glue a length of thin cord through and do the same at the butt: this is the safety cord that prevents the cork from flying too far. These

137

Carpet golf requires a miniature set of appropriate equipment: the holes are simply made from heavy wooden blocks that have a hole to take a marble, a small wooden or ping-pong ball; a slot or a ramp will help guide the ball home. One 1950s game incorporates a set of nine such ramps complete with hazards as in Crazy Golf. The size and construction of items of play is flexible, from the very small tabletop version to child size: it all depends on how much room you have.

Carpet bowls was very popular with the Victorians; real antique sets are made from real stone, heavy composition or even from ceramic, and they are usually decorated with a series of fine, tartan-like lines. You can easily produce a set by turning the bowls from hardwood - a heavy fruitwood such as cherry is ideal. Again, sizes all depend on how much room you have to play in. For the rules you will need to consult a regular player of the full-sized game or an appropriate book.

Blow Football became extremely popular during and just after the Second World War, when materials for toys were in very short supply. I remember a set with goals made from fencing wire, and tubes made from rolled cardboard as blowers, and I spent many a rainy hour happily playing this super game. You can make the game in lots of ways, and it is very easily done: all you need is two or more hollow bamboo or elder branch tubes, two goals made from scrap wood or from bent wire and a ping-pong ball. A dedicated pitch could be made from thin ply or MDF, but any flat tabletop will do. To prevent the ball rolling over the edge, surround it with model advertising signs made from wide strips of heavy card bent tent-like lengthways.

Blow football, a great wartime favourite that is so easy to make from found materials.

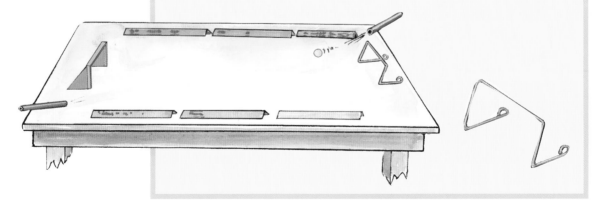

Bagatelle is an exciting board game played with marbles or steel ball-bearings, easily made from 9mm ply or MDF board. I am not aware of specific dimensions for the board, or for rules: I have seen many variations on the theme. Essentially, the board needs to be large enough to play on, say 100cm by 40cm, and rounded at the top end and edged all the way round to prevent the marbles rolling off. Fix a long block of wood underneath the top (curved) end to ensure that the balls roll into play once launched. At the very bottom of the board you can form a marble/cue store (with a lid) by adding extra strips of wood, leaving room on the right-hand side for another short strip that forms the narrow marble-launching area. Marbles are launched or struck into play by the use of a short dowel or turned cue. Alternatively you might like to make a spring-loaded plunger, the action of which can be supplied by a steel compression spring or a strong elastic band. The flat surface of the board has a series of ball catchers: these can be drilled shallow depressions, or just U-shaped rows of round-head brass nails. Each catch point is marked with a score valued according to difficulty and the scores can be

A simple bagatelle board, a game that can still be enjoyed today, note the detail showing two ways to make scoring cups, one just a hole and the other panel pins set in a deep curve to catch the marbles.

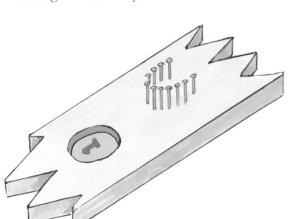

*Alternative ways to
make a spring launcher
for the bagatelle board,
you could of course
make a small cue as
used in snooker instead.*

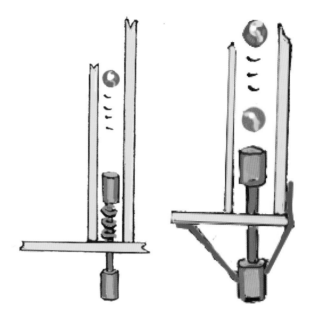

marked in tens or hundreds. The same round-head nails are used at various points around the board to act as baffles. It is surprising just how much the marbles bounce from one to the other in play: scoring is more by chance than by skill. Commercial boards have always been beautifully decorated and finished, but the homemade wartime boards I remember were very plain with the scores marked with ink or burned on with a red-hot wire. Players take turns to strike an agreed number of balls; the final scores are then added up to find the winner.

Architectural building blocks appeared around the end of the eighteenth century, and, followed in Victorian times by other wooden construction kits, they remain very popular today. Manufacturers have joined sets of wooden sticks or dowels together so that as many models can be constructed as possible. The colourful building blocks illustrated are a typical example: they stack together in all kinds ways. As a maker, experiment with blocks, discs and other shapes drilled all round with neatly spaced holes to take standard dowelling as a push-fit. This follows an idea of a toy maker from Illinois, USA, who was inspired by watching children thread wooden rods through cotton reels to invent and eventually patent the Tinkertoy, a clever construction set that used a whole variety of wooden shapes drilled all around to take hardwood dowelling. To promote the sets he employed midgets to demonstrate them in the window of a Chicago store, his clever publicity stunt making them so popular that he soon sold a million sets. Tinkertoys are considered collector's items nowadays, even though modern versions are available. Try experimenting with the manufacturer Crandall's idea of grooves and slots, or V or U-shaped notches as in Lincoln Logs. Flat lollipop sticks or specially prepared strips and shapes are wonderful for making into Meccano-like parts. Try a little lateral thinking: you may even come up with a world-beater to compete with these famous trade names from the past.

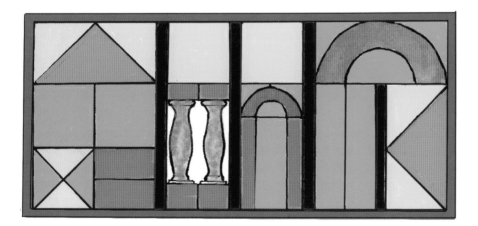

A boxed set of Victorian, architectural building blocks that would please any budding builder.

Marble Bridges

The wonderful game of Marbles Bridge seems to have appeared around the time of the Tudors; I have a book containing a contemporary engraving depicting a group of adults rolling marbles towards a rather fancy bridge with at least eight small numbered arches. This game is simple to make from almost any kind of board: use a large-diameter drill to make the curve, after which a pair of saw cuts complete the arch cut-outs. Look at my illustrations: you will see that the bridge can be cut to many profiles, the castle one being most effective. A very quick and easy version of the game can be made by simply cutting arches into one long side of a cardboard shoe box. You can make marbles easily and quickly from ordinary pottery clay (sometimes dug from the garden): just roll lumps of clay between the palms to produce suitable spheres. A short time in a hot oven or in the ashes of a bonfire or barbecue (children must be under supervision) will bake them hard enough to play with. An alternative to this would be to use modern, cool-bake modelling clay called Fimo. Clay marbles have a lovely eccentric way of rolling which makes play very interesting.

The game is educational for young children as they are required to do simple arithmetic. The rules are very easy. Ideally, three

Boys rolling balls or marbles down a ramp (Ancient Greece).

participants are best: one, the player, shares half the marbles (at least ten) with the bridge-keeper, while the third takes the part of referee and scorer; all take turns. The player kneels at least a metre away from the bridge, rolling his or her marbles one at a time in an attempt to get them through the numbered arches. If the player succeeds, the bridge-keeper must pay him or her the number of marbles indicated. But if any marble does not score, the bridge-keeper keeps that marble; in the meantime the referee is kept busy preventing any cheating while keeping score. Players take turns when all the marbles are lost by the player or bridge-keeper. You can have great fun in a school playground or hall by cutting large arches into the side of a long cardboard box. Ordinary tennis or play balls can be used instead of marbles.

Three ways of making a marbles bridge game, popular since Tudor times or even earlier.

Other Games

Many wooden games have been enjoyed for centuries, and most are very easy and cheap to make. **The Hobby-Horse** or **Stick-Horse** is one of the oldest wooden toys in history: accounts and pictures abound from all periods and all around the world. It is only in recent years that its appeal has diminished, but it can still be found. My illustration shows the hobby-horse in its many forms, such as a simple hedgerow stick, a walking stick, and many carved variations both with and without prancing forelegs - amazingly these were the only variations until the wheeled variety of the Victorians and later. Illustrations from early medieval times through to the late eighteenth century show young hobby-horse riders wielding stick mills as lances (see Windmills to Whirligigs). Remember that for thousands of years horses were

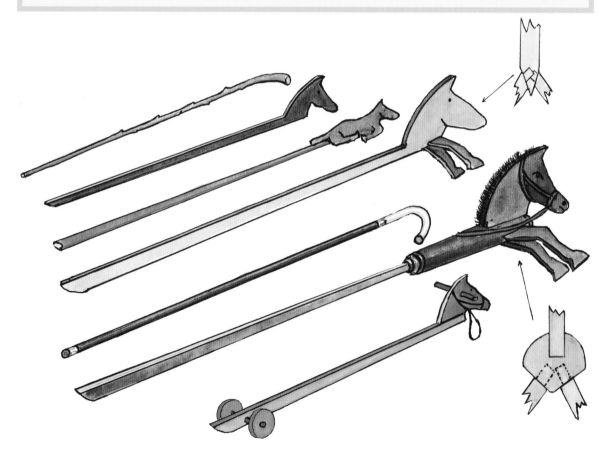

A composite drawing showing the historic development of the ubiquitous hobby or stick horse, they didn't have wheels until Victorian times. (See my black and white drawings.)

practically the only way to travel at any speed. Owning a hobby-horse was the equivalent of a modern child having a favourite model car.

Making a hobby-horse could not be simpler: a smooth, strong stick with a cut-out head in profile stuck firmly on to the end. The more adventurous operator might like to make the more complicated models illustrated. If you wish to add a pair of wheels I recommend you fix them so that they only just touch the ground when the stick is at the riding angle. This will prevent the annoying refusal of the horse to stand up for storage. Adding paint, a horsehair or fake fur mane and leather harness will add to the fun, as will putting cord-wrapped hilts and fake jewels on the weapons and painting bright heraldic designs on the shields. You can easily make a wonderful harness from discarded leather belts found in charity shops, all fixed with strong glue and shiny, dome-topped, brass upholstery nails. Medieval and Tudor children also liked to have mock battles with scaled-down wooden swords, shields and daggers (see line drawing). For safety, I recommend that all points be very rounded and blunt. Sensible children will not deliberately hurt one another, but adult supervision is advised for weapon play.

Fivestones is also one of the oldest recorded games: it was well known by the Ancient Greeks and the Romans, who played it using the knucklebones of sheep or goats. From medieval times onwards it seems that any five small items, such as pebbles, shells or

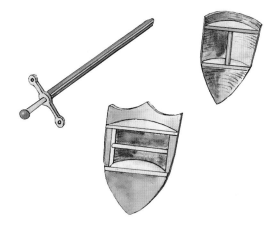

A wooden sword and two types of wooden shield, use history books for other ideas

Tudor and Medieval children with hobby horses and stick horses

147

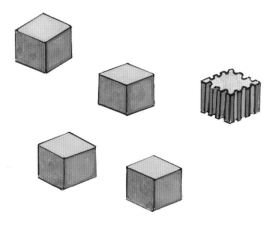

A set of typical five stones made from wooden cubes, note the one with grooves, these are formed on the strip of wood before cutting up into sections.

wooden blocks, were used. The Victorians introduced fivestones made from pottery, and during the Second World War the game enjoyed a great revival. Because materials were in short supply, manufacturers started to produce them in a soft, moulded (easily chipped) coloured chalk. The simple, homemade, wooden blocks surfaced again; those that were manufactured, whether from chalk or wood, had distinctive grooves running down four edges (see illustration). Fivestones continues to this day. The game can be made by cutting a square section rod of hardwood into exact cubes; the dimensions will vary according to whether the sets are for adult or child use. To make the wooden fivestones more interesting (and to improve catching), three fine grooves can be machined on to all four faces of the strip before it is cut up. Each small block must be sanded smooth all round, and they look better if they are stained or painted in bright colours before use.

In Britain fivestones has been extremely popular in playgrounds and pavements over the years, and has been known by many other names, depending on location, such as Snobs (Leicestershire and Derbyshire), Alley Gobs (London), Chucks and Pot Checks (Lancashire). Other names include Kibs, Bobber, Chuckies, Clinks, Dibs and Dabs. Because of its long history, there are no specific rules for playing fivestones but most people over sixty will be able to remember theirs. Have fun finding out: you will be amazed at the variety of increasingly difficult throws and catches there are. Ask about clicks and no clicks, snatch, ones, twos and threes, and so on. I am sure that if a large company produced fivestones sets with flashing lights and buzzers the game would soon regain its popularity. I can just imagine a fivestones craze: they beat X-Box any day. After the end of the Second World War, when metal for toy production was made available, we were able to buy shiny, star-shaped fivestones, also known as Jacks. Metal jacks introduced a small rubber ball into the fivestones game; I never played this but I believe sets are still available from specialist shops and market stalls.

Please explore the Brueghel's painting on pages 66-67, see if you can find the children playing knucklebones (fivestones).

Sword and shield play from a medieval print.

Optical Toys

The Victorians loved toys that could teach as well as entertain: steam models, flying toys, educational board and card games were top sellers in all the best toyshops. Optical toys featured high on the list, and most had hard-to-pronounce names taken from the Greek, such as Thaumatrope, Zoetrope, Pilkington Pedemascope, Praxinoscope, and so on. All relied on the scientific discovery of the persistence of vision when the human eye is tricked into seeing apparently moving images when a series of pictures is flashed in front of the eyes. The Zoetrope and Praxinoscope are too complicated for inclusion in this book, but the Thaumatrope and the Pilkington Pedemascope are easily made from workshop scraps.

The Thaumatrope is the simplest, made from circles of thick card. A more permanent set can be made from circles cut from thin ply or MDF board. Cut a set of circles at least 6cm in diameter; next, sandpaper until smooth all round the edges, then drill small holes on opposite sides to take thin cord lops (see illustration). Paint the circles in any pale background colour. Now for the artistic bit: on one side of a circle draw and colour a goldfish, then a bowl (upside down) on the other side. When the cords are twirled between fingers and thumbs the disc revolves and, as if by magic, the goldfish appears in his bowl. Now experiment with different pairs of pictures, such as a bird and cage or a lady in a window. Another way is to make just one plain wooden circle, then cut a whole set of circles

The two sides of a Victorian Thaumatrope optical toy that is so easy to make from wood or suitable card.

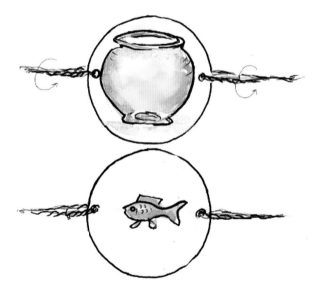

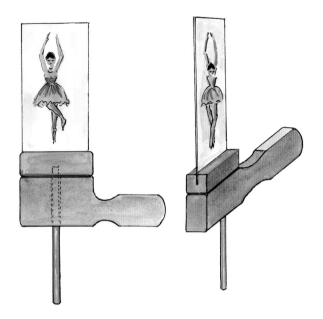

from card. Use tiny dabs of Blu-Tack or similar adhesive putty to hold them temporarily while spun on the Thaumatrope. In this case, you will need a pair of card circles for each design.

Similar semi-rotation is the key to using the **Pilkington Pedemascope**, an optical toy invented by a Mr Pilkington in 1869. It consists of a simple, shallow, L-shaped holder cut from 1cm-thick board. After cutting and sanding, drill a thin hole centrally upwards, then separate the rectangular top portion with a fine saw. Groove the top of this to take a set of thin cards, as shown. Glue a short length of 3mm dowel into the underside of the revolving top; then drill a slightly larger hole through the handle so that the dowel and top can revolve freely. Colour simple drawings (or use computer Clip Art) on both sides of each card, ensuring that the one on the back differs slightly from the one on the front. When you place a card in the groove and semi-rotate it between finger and thumb via the dowel, the picture will appear to move.

A little more sophisticated but easy to make is the **Stroboscope** or **Phenakistoscope**, a simpler version of the Zoetrope and Praxinoscope. The phenakistoscope consists of a thin circle of thin board around 20cm in diameter that has a series of slots cut out all around its circumference. There should be ten equally spaced slots all about 4cm long by 3mm wide; they can be cut in from the edge or slotted with a router or side-cutting drill. The whole disc is carefully sanded all round, then mounted on a

A Victorian Phenakistoscope optical toy that utilises a mirror.

handle so that it revolves easily around a central screw. A set of card circles is cut to fit the inner diameter of the slots. As with the Pedemascope, the circular cards can be temporarily stuck with Blu-Tack. Under each slot draw a picture that changes slightly as you go round. To see the pictures move you need to stand in front of a mirror, holding the handle with the pictures facing the mirror. Look through the slots at the reflected images: as you revolve the disc you will be amazed to see the pictures come to life.

All of the above optical toys were the forerunners of cinema cartoon animation and moving pictures in general, both of which we take for granted today.

Second World War Toys

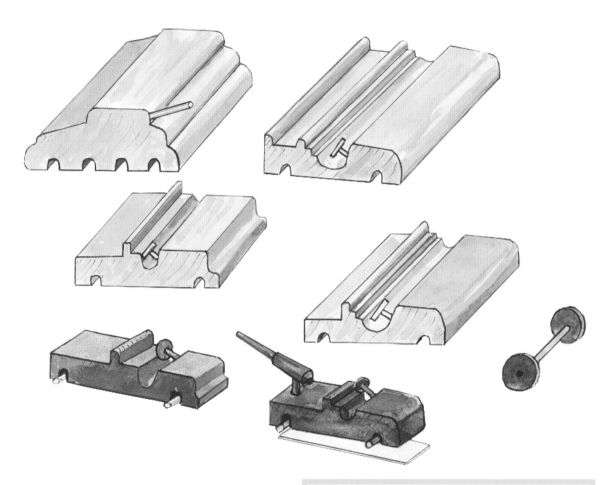

Details of how a 1940s American company produced a whole series of WWII vehicles by machining continuous profiles in a similar way to 19th Century German toy makers.

I place these in a separate category because the years of the Second World War brought wooden toys unexpectedly back to the fore. As I described in the Introduction, essential materials such as metals, rubber and plastics were required for the war effort, and toy manufacturers were made to produce aircraft or vehicle parts, weapons and even wooden crates. To keep up morale they were allowed to produce restricted quantities of cheaply made cardboard, paper and wooden games, while wartime children made their own toys from the hedgerow or from scraps, usually with help from grandparents who recalled their own Victorian or Edwardian childhoods. I well remember getting help making whistles, bows and arrows, cotton reel tanks, tip-cats, catapults, pea-shooters, wooden swords and guns.

In the USA, the Jaymar Speciality Company produced boxed sets of Midgie toys of a very

During the severe restrictions on materials many toys during WWII were made from wood, like this American machine-gun.

clever design. These beautiful toys featured in most major wholesale catalogues of the time. The tiny wooden military jeeps, tanks, armoured cars, aircraft and field guns reflected the ongoing conflict. Printed cardboard tents and paper flags added to their realism, enough to spark the imaginations of wartime children. The tiny aircraft and gun barrels were lathe-turned, and all the vehicles were cut from long lengths of specially machined profile strips. Almost a throwback to the slicing of Noah's Ark animals from turned profiles in nineteenth-century Germany. Look closely at the pictures (page 154) and you will see how quickly those little vehicles could be made once the profile-cutting spindle moulders were set up for full production. I have quite a few in my collection; I can only admire the ingenuity of their designers, especially how simple grooves covered by strong cardboard bases keep wheels and axles in place. The aircraft wings, flags and propellers are all

During the 19th Century German toy makers lathe turned circular profiles of Ark and farm animals, then individual animals would be split off ready for carving and painting..

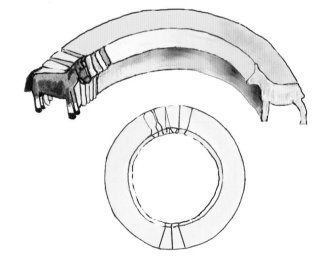

made from card or paper. I include here details of a clever way of producing dozens of identical wheeled vehicles. Access to, and knowledge of, woodworking machinery is essential to produce them, although simpler profiles could be produced with a router or even hand planes. Once you have cut the chosen profile(s), saw off short sections then sand and decorate them to produce vehicle sets. The wheels are cleverly held in place by gluing on the base card; the addition of steering-wheels, guns, searchlights, and so on, add to the variations. An excellent example of how shortage of materials can turn lateral thinking into profit.

The rasping-noise-making cog mechanism of the rotary rattle formed an essential part of the toy machine guns, Tommy guns and Sten guns of the period. Similarly, elastic band power came to the fore to produce matchstick-firing cannon or torpedo-firing model submarines and patrol boats. The American Craft 50 Cal. Raider automatic weapon pictured is based on the one in my collection. Many weapons of this type were also made at home by servicemen on leave or recovering from battle wounds. Many other wartime toys were produced by German and Italian POWs for pocket money - it was very strange for us children to receive toys from former enemies. And, as mentioned, many Victorian and Edwardian toys and games enjoyed a strong revival in the early 1940s thanks to loving grandparents who recreated the toys they had known in childhood.

Conclusion

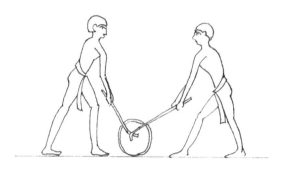

Boys with a hoop and sticks (Ancient Egypt).

My task is complete. I trust that you have enjoyed reading the book. I sincerely hope that you made at least one of the toys featured. I realize that there are many items that I have missed, but I had to stop somewhere. My aim has been to promote a lasting interest in wooden toys, dolls and games and I feel strongly that I have given my readers a head start. I am always interested in any old and unusual wooden toy, doll or game, especially if it has not been included here.

Cyril Hobbins
Toy Maker of Kenilworth

Postscript

Three boys riding stick horses, note that one horse is a walking stick.

Like the wooden piles and foundations supporting the dwellings and footpaths of old you must agree that traditional wooden toys also helped to lay the foundations of human development and civilisation?

Cyril Hobbins 2006

Bibliography

Adams, Morley, *You Can Make It*, London, Faber and Faber, 1942

Adburgham, Alison, *Gamages Christmas Bazaar*, London, David and Charles, 1974

Alton, W. G., *Wooden Toys That You Can Make*, London, Mills and Boon, 1972

Anders, Lunde, *Whirligigs for Children*, Radnor, Chilton, 1992

Auerbach, Stevanne, *The Toy Chest*, Ontario, General, 1986

Auerbach, Stevanne, *Toys Smart: How to Raise a Child with a High PQ*, New York, St Martins Griffin, 1998

Auerbach, Stevanne and Schwarz, *Toys for a Lifetime*, New York, Byron Preiss, 1999

Bachmann, Manfred, *German Toys 1924-1926*, Cumberland, Hobby House, 1985

Bachmann, Manfred and Hansmann, Claus, *Dolls the World Over: An Historical Account*, London, Harrap, 1973

Baker, Roger, *Dolls and Dolls' Houses*, London, Orbis, 1973

Barlow, Ronald S., *The Great American Antique Toy Bazaar 1879-1945*, California, Windmill, 1998

Baten, Lea, *Japanese Folk Toys*, Tokyo, Shufunotomo, 1992

Batsford, B. T. and Fraser, Antonia, *A History of Toys*, London, Weidenfeld and Nicolson, 1966

Beaumont, Cyril, Puppets and Puppetry, London, The Studio, 1958

Becket, Geoffrey and MacGregor, Elizabeth, *Amusing the Children*, Maidenhead, Sampson Low, 1975

Medieval youth with a three vaned egg mill and a girl wearing a willow hat whilst blowing a hedgerow whistle and shaking a rattle. Ref: Brueghel.

Bibliography

Bell, R. C., *Board and Table Games for All The Family*, London, Penguin, 1988

Bell, R. C., *The Board Game Book*, London, Marshall Cavendish, 1979

Bestelmeier-Katalog, Zurich, Olms, 1979

Blizzard, Richard, *Making Wooden Toys*, London, John Murray, 1983

Blizzard, Richard, *More of Blizzard's Wooden Toys*, London, BBC, 1987

Bloomfield, Ron and Stephenson, Audrey, *Making Toys*, London, BBC, 1977

Bridgewater, Alan and Gill, *Making Noah's Ark Toys in Wood*, New York, Sterling, 1988

Bridgewater, Alan and Gill, *Popular Crafts Guide to Making Wooden Toys that Move*, London, Argus, 1986

Bridgewater, Alan and Gill, *The Wonderful World of Whirligigs and Wind Machines*, Blue Ridge Summit, Tab, 1990

Burda, Cindy, *Wind Toys*, New York, Sterling, 1999

Burke, J., Nevile, F., Fuller, R. and Garrood, D., *Make Your Own Wooden Toys*, London, Windward, W. H. Smith/Marshall Cavendish, 1987

Bussell, Jan, *The Puppet Theatre*, London, Faber and Faber, 1946

Cadbury, Betty, *Playthings Past*, London, David and Charles, 1976

Calder, Andrew, *The Toy Maker*, London, Wolfe, 1976

Camm, F. J. (ed.), Hobbies New Annual, London, George Newnes, 1920

Catford, Nancy, *Making Nursery Toys*, London, Frederick Muller, 1944 and London, Elek, 1969

Cieslik, Jürgen and Marianne, Lehmann Toys: *The History of EP Lehmann 1881-1981*, tr. Barrows Massey, London, New Cavendish, 1982

Boy holding a jousting mill whilst riding a hobby horse.

160

Coleman, Dorothy S., Elizabeth A. and Evelyn, *The Collector's Encyclopedia of Dolls (Vol I)*, London, Robert Hale, 1970

Country Treasures Worked in Wood, New York, Sedgewood, 1989

Cowper, William, *The Diverting History of John Gilpin*, London, Penguin, 1954

Coxon, John, *Easy to Make Learning Toys*, New York, Sterling, 1987

Creighton, Ellen R.C., *Ellen Buxton's Journal 1860-1864*, London, Bles, 1967

Crooke-Parry, Charlotte, *Toys, Dolls and Games (Paris 1903-1914)*, London, 1981

Culff, Robert, *The World of Toys*, Middlesex, Hamlyn, 1969

Daiken, Leslie, *Children's Toys Throughout the Ages*, London, Batsford, 1953 and London, Spring, 1965

Dalby, Stuart, *Making Model Buildings*, Poole, Blandford, 1980

Danby, Hal, *Make Your Own Toys and Games*, London, Fontana, 1979

Darbyshire, Lydia, *The Collector's Encyclopedia of Toys and Dolls*, London, Quintet, 1990

Dinneen, John, *Marbles, Hopscotch and Jacks: Favourite Games and Variations*, London, Angus and Robertson, 1987

Doll Collectors Manual, Maryland, Hobby Horse, 1983

Douet, Valerie Jackson, *World Guide to Dolls*, London, Apple Press, 1993

Eaton, Faith, *Care and Repair of Antique and Modern Dolls*, Poole, Blandford, 1985

Encyclopedia of Sports, Games and Pastimes, London, Fleet, circa 1935

Evec, Janet, Puppetry, London, Foyle, 1952

A charming illustration of a young girl being given instructions on the use of a Diablo.

Bibliography

Fairhurst, Peter, *Making Model Aeroplanes*, London, Carousel, 1983

Farnworth, Warren, *Folk Toys and How to Make Them*, London, Chatto and Windus, 1974

Favorite, Mary J. and Engler, Nick, *Country Woodworking*, New York, Sedgewood, 1990

Fawdry, Kenneth and Marguerite, *Pollock's History of English Dolls and Toys*, Enderby, Promotional Reprint,1993

Fawdry, Marguerite, *English Rocking Horses*, London, Pollock's Toy Theatres, 1986

Fletcher, Jill Helen, *The Big Book of Things to Do and Make*, London, Odhams, 1972

Flick, Pauline, *Old Toys*, California, Shire, 1987

Ford, Marion, *Copy Cats*, London, Andre Deutsch, 1983

Fraser, Antonia, *Dolls*, London, Octopus, 1963

Freeman, Philip and Sayer, Caroline, *Making Victorian Kinetic Toys*, New York, Taplinger, 1977

Garratt, John G., *Model Soldiers: A Collector's Guide*, Moscow, Seeley Service, 1959

Goodfellow, Caroline, *The Ultimate Doll Book*, London, Dorling Kindersley, 1993

Gould, D. W., *The Top: Universal Toy, Enduring Pastime*, New York, Clarkson N. Potter, 1973

Gray, David and Ilse, *Stay Indoors Book*, London, Studio Vista, 1975

Grober, Karl, *Children's Toys of Bygone Days*, London, Batsford, 1932

Hall, Dorothea, *Memories of Childhood (Everyday Collectibles)*, London, W. H. Smith/Marshall Cavendish, 1990

Hall, Sylvia, *How to Make Dolls*, Leicester, Ladybird, 1978

Handicrafts Annual, London, Odhams, 1933

An 18th Century boy on a grand hobby horse.

Haskell, Arnold and Lewis, Min, *Infantilia: The Archaeology of the Nursery*, London, Dennis Dobson, 1971

Haslam, Fred, *Small Toys in Wood*, London, Evans Brothers, circa 1942

Hayward, Charles H., *Making Toys in Wood*, London, Evans Brothers, 1963

Hersey, Marcia, *Collecting Baby Rattles and Teethers*, Iola, Krause, 1998

Hillier, Mary, *Dolls and Dollmakers*, London, Weidenfeld and Nicolson, 1968

Hoke, Helen and Pels, Walter, *Toys*, London, Dobson, 1971

Holler, Rene, *Kreisel (Tops)*, Munich, Hugendubel, 1989

Holler, Rene, *Murmeln (Marbles)*, Munich, Hugendubel, 1995

Holme, Geoffrey C., *Children's Toys of Yesterday*, London, The Studio, 1932

Holz, Loretta, *The How To Book of International Dolls*, New York, Crown, 1980

Home Hobbies in Wood, London, Evans, circa 1942

Horth, Arthur C., 101 *Games to Make and Play*, London and Worcester, Batsford, 1946

Hsiao, P., Lorimer, N. and Williams, N., *Games You Can Make and Play*, London, Macdonald and Janes, 1975

Irving, Richard, *Wooden Toymaking Step by Step*, London, Frederick Warne, 1961

Jackson, Mrs F. Nevill, *Toys of Other Days*, London, Newnes, 1950 and London, White Lion, 1975

Joseph, Joan, *Folk Toys Around the World*, New York, Parents Magazine Press, 1972

Kandert, Dr Josef, *The World of Toys*, London,

A 19th Century French girl playing 'Bilboquet' or cup and ball.

Bibliography

Hamlyn Octopus Illustrated, 1992

Kay, J. and White, C. T., *Toys: Their Design and Construction*, Kent, University of London Press, 1945

Kenneway, Eric, *Fingers Knuckles and Thumbs*, London, Hamlyn, 1978

Kenneway, Eric, *Magic, Toys, Tricks and Illusions*, London, Arrow, 1987

Ketchum, W. C., *Toys and Games*, Washington, Smithsonian Institution, 1981

Kevill-Davies, Sally, *Yesterday's Children and History of Childcare*, Suffolk, Antique Collectors Club, 1994

King, Constance Eileen, *Dolls and Dolls' Houses*, London, Chancellor, 1996

King, Constance Eileen, *The Encyclopedia of Toys*, London, New Burlington, 1985

King, Constance Eileen, *Toys and Dolls for Collectors*, London, Hamlyn, 1973

McLaughlin, Terence, *Working Toys and Models*, London, Pelham, 1977

Mackay, James, *Nursery Antiques*, London, Ward Lock, 1976

Manistree, H. E., *Help Yourself Handbook: Aircraft Carrier*, Dredger, London, Cassell, 1959

Manistree, H. E., *Help Yourself Handbook: Helicopter, Spaceship*, London, Cassell, 1959

Manistree, H. E., *Help Yourself Handbook: Stagecoach, Rocket*, London, Cassell, 1959

Miller, Lynn, *Toy Making*, London, Pittman, 1952

Millet, Marion, *Working Wooden Toys*, New York, Sterling and London, Blandford, 1985, 1986, 1987

Mullins, Patricia, *The Rocking Horse*, London, New Cavendish, 1992

Murphy, Bruce and Lopo, Ana, *Lampmaking*, New York, Sterling, 1980

A Tudor girl holding a costumed Bartholomew Baby and a beautifully made crib.

Nelson, John R., *American Folk Toys*, Newtown, Taunton, 1998

Opie, Iona and Robert, and Anderson, Brian, *The Treasures of Childhood*, London, Pavilion/Michael Joseph, 1989

Opie, James, *Collecting Toy Soldiers*, London, New Cavendish, 1987 and Tampa, Pincushion, 1992

Page, Hilary, *Toys in Wartime London*, George Allen and Unwin, 1942

Peduzzi, Anthony and Judy, *Making Moving Wooden Toys*, Newton Abbot and London, David and Charles, 1985

Peppe, Rodney, *Rodney Peppe's Moving Toys*, London, Evans Brothers, 1980

Pickles, Rennie and Pat, *Jig Dolls: The Brightest of Entertainers*, Wakefield, Pickles, circa 1986

Picot, P. and Rohan, M. S., *Making Toys from Tins*, tr. A. F. Hartley, Wakefield, E. P., 1982

Pierce, Sharon, *Making Holiday Folktoys and Figures*, New York, Sterling, 1987

Pierce, Sharon, *Making Old Time Folk Toys*, New York, Sterling, 1986

Pierce, Sharon, *Making Whirligigs and other Wind Toys*, New York, Sterling, 1985

Pieske, Christa, *Schönes Spielzeug*, Munich, Morion, 1984

Polkinghome, R. K. and M. I. R., *Toymaking in School and Home*, London, Harrap, 1916, 1917, 1921, 1925 and 1930

Pollock, *Pollock's History of English Dolls and Toys*, London, Benn, 1979

Reichardt, Jasia, *Play Orbit*, London, Studio International, 1969

Robson, D., *Rainy Day Kites and Flying Objects*, London, Aladdin/Franklin Watts, 1991

18th Century children with a hoop.

Bibliography

Rocard, Anne, *Puppets and Marionettes*, Wakefield, E. P., 1981

Röttger, Ernst, *Creative Woodcraft 2*, London, Batsford, 1960

Rowland, T. J. S., *Everyday Things for Lively Youngsters*, London, Cassell, 1941

Schnack, Dick, *American Folk Toys: How to Make Them*, Middlesex, Penguin, 1985

Schoonmaker, David and Woods, Bruce, *Whirligigs and Weathervanes*, New York, Sterling, 1991

Sibbett, Ed, *Wooden Puzzle Toys: Patterns and Instructions*, New York, Dover, 1978

Sidcum, Jerry and Botermans, Jack, *Puzzles Old and New: How to Make and Solve*, Wellingborough, Thorsons, 1987

Simmen, Rene, *The World of Puppets*, London, Elsevier Phaidon, 1975

Slade, Richard, *Toys From Balsa*, London, Faber and Faber, 1946

Smith, Edward, *How to Make Action Toys*, New York, Smith Brook, 1988

Smith, Roland G., *First Models in Cardboard*, Leicester, Dryad, 1969

Snook, Barbara, *Puppets*, Leicester, Dryad, 1985

Soloviova, Larissa, *Russian Matryoshka*, Moscow, Interbook, 1993

Sommer, Robert Langley, *Toys of Our Generation: Post-War Collectibles 1945-1974*, Wigston, Magna, 1992

Stirn, Carl P., *Turn of the Century Dolls, Toys, Games*, New York, Dover/Henry Ford Museum, 1990

Studley, Vance, *The Woodworker's Book of Wooden Toys*, New York, Van Nostrand Reinhold, 1980

Taylor, Kerry, The Collector's Guide to Dolls,

15th Century youth bowling a large hoop.

London, Bracken, 1995

The Boys' Own Toy Maker, Racine, Johnson-Smith

The Story of Games and Toys, circa 1935

Things to Do and Make, London, Reader's Digest, 1977

Thomson, Neil and Ruth, *Fairground Games to Make and Play*, London, Marshall Cavendish, 1977

Viney, Nigel and Grant, Neil, *An Illustrated History of Ball Games*, London, Book Club, 1978

White, Gwen, *Antique Toys*, London, Chancellor, 1971

White, Gwen, *European and American Dolls*, London, Chancellor, 1966

Whittaker, Nicholas, *Toys Were Us*, London, Orion, 2001

Wickers, David and Finmark, Sharon, *How You Can Make Your Own Kinetics*, London, Studio Vista, 1972

Williams, Ursula Moray, *Adventures of the Little Wooden Horse*, London, Puffin, 1959

Men with Yo-Yo's from an 18th Century print.

Gallery

Top left: A two weight balancer Folk Toy circa 1950.
Top Middle: A policeman Pantin or Hamplemann circa 1980.
Top right: A cowboy single weight balancer circa 1990.
Bottom left: Pecking chickens on a board/paddle 1940s.
Bottom right: Pantin/Hamplemann 18th Century design (a replica).

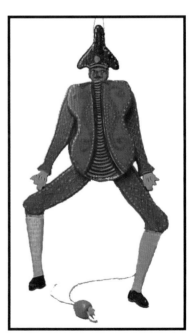

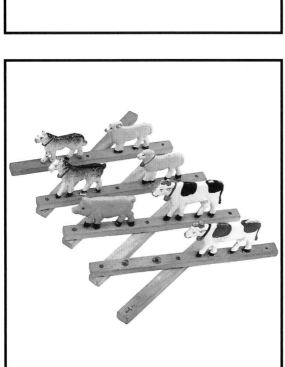

Top left: A little jointed poseable toy dog (Victorian).

Bottom left: A scissors action toy with farm animals (Victorian).

Right: A large balancing parrot circa 1930.

Top left: Two examples of push pull toys.

Top right: A tumbler clown on his stand.

Middle: A catch toy with two cups plus a wooden spring action (Portugal).

Bottom: A traditional push pull toy from Sweden.

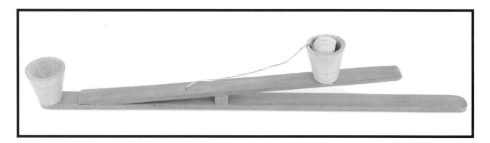

Top: A finger spinning top figure from Japan.

Middle left: A peg wooden or Dutch doll (Victorian).

Middle, centre: Tudor Bartholomew Babies or stump dolls (Ref: Museum of London Tudor Stuart Department).

Bottom: A Poupard stump doll with traditionally painted swaddling clothes (French 19th Century) replica.

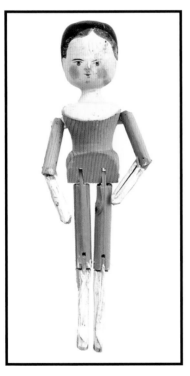

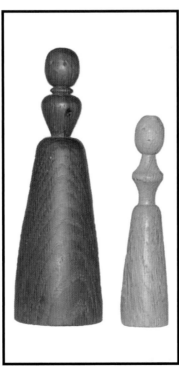

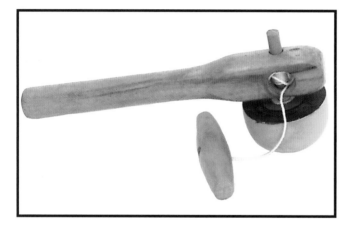

Top left: A whirligig horse (replica).

Middle right: A cord pull launcher top from Japan.

Middle left: An egg or nut mill with three revolving vanes (Ref: Brughel).

Bottom: A horn book battledore and shuttlecock set (replicas).

Top left: A whip top also known as a window breaker or a granny top.

Top right:
A cuckoo-call whistle whittled from a hedgerow branch (Author).
And another one with a bird made in the traditional German manner.

Bottom left: A flipping or jumping frog.

Bottom right: The dastardly snake-in-a-box trick (authors version).

Bottom: A traditional bean shooter folk toy from the Appalachian Mountains USA.

Index

Index

Index

Index